99 Things Women Wish

They Knew Before®…

Starting Their Own Business

A woman's guide to avoiding
start-up disasters

Erica Diamond

www.99-series.com

The 99 Series
600 Brunet
Montreal, QC H4M1X8
Canada

323-203-0548

First published by The 99 Series 2010

Cover design and layout by **Ginger Marks**,
DocUmeantDesigns
www.DocUmeantDesigns.com

Copy Editor Allister Thompson **Alter Editorial Services**
www.altereditorialservices.com

Distributed by DocUmeant Publishing

For inquiries about volume orders, please contact:

Helen Georgaklis
99 Book Series, Inc.
600 Brunet Avenue
Montreal, Quebec
Canada
H4M 1X8

Helen@99-series.com

Printed in the United States Of America
ISBN-13: 978-0-9866923-0-7 9.99 (paperback)
ISBN-10: 0986692301

WORDS OF PRAISE

FOR...

---

99 Things Women Wish They Knew Before®... Starting Their Own Business

"Erica embodies one of the greatest things about women: multi-tasking. She has accomplished so much, conquering the fields of business, parenting, blogging, and also contributing to charity work. Women should draw inspiration from her and especially from this book: be bold! There is nothing you cannot do if you put your mind and heart into it."

Sarah Ferguson, *Duchess of York*

"There's a saying that Ginger Rogers did everything Fred Astaire did, but backwards and in high heels...we women are multi-taskers. Whether you're one of the many Women on the Fence that Erica Diamond has captivated with her blog, or you're simply a woman with an entrepreneurial spirit who wants someone to guide you through the pitfalls and triumphs of starting your own business, you will love this book. Erica is passionate, and her passion will rub off on you. Every woman needs a plan to realize her potential, and this book will motivate you to start moving in the right direction."— **Brooke Burke,** *Co-CEO of ModernMom.com and Co-Host of ABC's "Dancing With the Stars"*

"If you're looking for a savvy entrepreneur to coach you through starting your own business, you need to read this book! Erica offers you the best advice that most people just don't! Erica's 99 tips are not only easy to follow...they actually work! You'll benefit from Erica's own experiences to see how to build the business you've always dreamed of and

write your own success story."—**Howard Starr,** *former CEO (1994-2009), Tommy Hilfiger Canada*

"For women to be successful in business, we have to juggle it all. If you're a woman with a passion to start a business, or even if you already have a business and are simply looking for great sales and marketing strategies, Erica can tell you how to start that business (and be a booming success) without leaving the rest of your life behind. You don't have to stifle your entrepreneurial spirit...with Erica cheering you on, you can achieve limitless success in business and life." —**Susan Mulder,** *Principal, McKinsey and Company*

"Erica Diamond is a breath of fresh air for the female. She embodies a spirit that is inspirational to all women who hold the desire to accomplish more in their lives. In 99 Things Women Wish They Knew Before...Starting Their Own Business, *Erica gives you the tools and tips to turn your dreams into reality. Whether it is learning about how to market your business, sell*

yourself or how to have it all and still maintain a personal life, you will learn and easily adopt her secrets to proven success. This book is much more than your average "Start your own Business" book, it is simply 99 things that WILL make a difference in your life. So...what are you waiting for? Start reading and get your business started!"

—Heidi Androl, *former NBC TV Show Apprentice Candidate and Producer/ Reporter for The Los Angeles Kings, Fox Sports West and the National Hockey League*

DEDICATION

This book is dedicated to all the incredibly supportive people who have stood by me throughout my journey. You are my air, my breath, my reason for living. And there are many. After all, it takes a village to raise a child.

CONTENTS

CHAPTER 6

GROW YOUR SALES QUICKLY   **91**

CHAPTER 7

DEVELOP THE "KILLER" MARKETING PLAN   **109**

ABOUT THE 99

SERIES

The 99 Series is a collection of quick, easy-to-understand guides that spell it all out for you in the simplest format; 99 points, one lesson per page. The book series is the one-stop shop for all readers tired of looking all over for self-help books. The 99 Series brings it all to you under one umbrella! The bullet point format that is the basis for all the 99 Series books was created purposely for today's fast-paced society. Not only does information have to be at our finger tips... we need it quickly and accurately without having to do much research to find it. But don't be fooled by the easy-to-read format. Each of the books in the series contains very thorough discussions from our roster of professional authors so that all the information you need to know is compiled into one book!

We hope that you will enjoy this book as well as the rest of the series. If you've enjoyed our books, tell your friends. And if you feel we need to improve something, please feel free to give us your feedback at www.99-series.com.

Helen Georgaklis
Founder & CEO, 99 Series

PREFACE

On April 7, 1975, I was born to two incredibly wonderful, doting parents. My early memories are of my mother and I—always together, always talking. I was constantly being nurtured. My father was out hunting to provide for his family, all the while fighting his insecurities as a result of growing up lacking many resources at home and having to help his family financially at a young age.

My parents were polar opposites. My mother, a teacher and therapist, was calm and rational. My father was an astute businessman, people person, and lover of life. But they were a unified front when it came to raising me. I was taught the value of a dollar early. Whenever I received my allowance, it was half to spend and half to save. As a child, I played at entrepreneurship. Each day I would play in the basement with my dolls (I had no siblings). I would develop a new business idea each day—opening a restaurant, designing clothing, or simply selling something. I loved sales. Moreover, I was given every encouragement to work hard and to chase my dreams.

Fast forward to my twenties. I had just graduated McGill University with a major in Psychology and an undeclared minor in Marketing. I was going the business route. My plan after graduation: get a great job for 2 years, and then return to MBA School. The great job came. MBA School didn't. I BOMBED my GMATs and found myself rejected from MBA School. I was DEVASTATED. I speak in this book about always having a Plan B. At the time, I had no Plan B, only a Plan A. But God had a Plan B in store for me that was far greater than anything I could have dreamed up myself.

I took being rejected from MBA School as a sign. I thought, "Now is the time to finally live my dream of entrepreneurship!" I was 24, and I was still living at home. I had saved up quite a bit of money, and against everyone's advice, I went for it! I cashed out $5,000 worth of investments, put up a website, made some ugly business cards, and got on a plane for The New York Gift Show. I was going into business for myself, and no one could stop me. Despite everyone asking me why I would enter the already competitive marketplace of promotional products, I knew I had it in me to make my venture a success. I returned home from the gift show with my samples in my suitcase, and I called everyone I knew.

On August 23, 1999, I registered my company for $37.00 and never once looked back. I worked up until the minute my water broke at 37 weeks pregnant in 2003. I was back in the office 48 hours later, pounding the pavement again. No maternity leave. Well, two days actually.

I owned my own business, and there was no maternity leave for business owners at the time. I continued to push hard. I won numerous business awards along the way and accomplished many milestones and much success.

In 2006, I was pregnant again, and an opportunity fell into my hands. Canada's largest retail chain for bags was courting me to purchase my business, and it was an offer I simply couldn't refuse. I knew that I was entrepreneurial in spirit, and that I would be merely taking a break for a while to raise my kids. It was a great 3 years at home with my boys that I feel gave them the foundation and confidence to set them on their way (much like my own mother had given me).

Fast forward to September 2009. I was getting restless at home, and I felt a little unfulfilled. My volunteer work was wonderful, but not nearly stimulating enough. Despite having written three children's books and a TV show while at home for those three years, my dream to connect with women around the world was so strong, so palpable, I couldn't deny it. I had a constant voice in my head and this burning desire to speak up and help inspire women to live their dreams. I couldn't quiet those voices. Hence the birth of my Women On The Fence Blog (WomenOnTheFence.com). Now women come from all around the world by the thousands to feel connected and inspired, to better understand their own life experiences, to laugh, and to cry. I urge them, as I do you ladies, to unlock their passion, get off the fence, and live their dreams. I am living proof two times over that it's completely possible to dream it, and then live it. And live it large.

While I have achieved great success over the past 11 years of being an entrepreneur, I have also made a lot of mistakes along the way. I hope to pass on the knowledge to you so that you don't repeat the ones I have made. I also figured out a few great tricks along the way, which I hope to pass on as well. Therefore, this guide is just that: YOUR

GUIDE. It is not a step-by-step plan to starting your own business. You can pick that up at your local bookstore. Instead this is a coach in a pocket. I am here as your business mentor and your coach to help guide you through the start-up phase of your business. If you are thinking of starting your own business, there are things you MUST KNOW to ensure your new venture is a huge success. We women have to stick together, and it is my goal to share my knowledge with you. I say it in my blog, and I'll say it here.

We're women. We are bright. We are dynamic. We are educated. We are perfectionists. We are tired. We love our husbands. We hate our husbands. We love our kids. Our kids annoy us. We want to work. We can't juggle it all. We expect two dozen roses on our anniversary. We give. We get. We're happy. We're discouraged. We're intuitive. We're funny.

We're women. Black. White. Asian. Hispanic. Through it all, we stick together.

Enjoy this guide. I wish you all the success in the world in starting your new venture. What an incredible opportunity! What an incredible journey it will be.

xoxEDxox

ACKNOWLEDGMENTS

To my parents Rosalie and Gary, who have loved me unconditionally and with such intensity. You have instilled in me the value of hard work and integrity since my inception. You are my sounding board, my strength and my inspiration. We're a small family, but we're a good family. Words cannot express my love for the two biggest role models and mentors in my life.

To my in-laws Harriet and Ron, who have treated me as their very own daughter since the day I met them. You never, ever laughed when I said I was going for my dreams. You have been always supportive, always an arm to lean on. I couldn't have asked for a better and warmer set of second parents. I love you both.

To Vangie for allowing me go to work all those years and now, without a worry. To know that my boys are safe at home with you, I feel lucky. You are like our fifth family member.

To my girlfriends. You girls simply do not realize how much you have given me in every way. Growing up an only child, you have truly been my sisters. I love you, my girlfriends, my best friends.

To my two boys. I dedicate this book to you. You are the reason I have accomplished so much. You keep me grounded and real. There is not a day that goes by that I don't learn one of life's lessons from you. I am so proud of the young boys you are becoming. If I had to do it all over again, even though I was praying for pink, I wouldn't have changed a single thing. Promise me that even when you go off and marry one day, you'll still stay close to Mommy. I love you to the depth and breadth and height my soul can reach.

To my wonderful and supportive husband, Hilly. I couldn't have done ANY OF THIS without you. I knew the minute I laid eyes on you at 17, even though you had a girlfriend at the time, that we would be together. You are my strength, my rock, my lover and my best friend. I can't imagine walking this earth without you. We've been through it all, and through it all together, side by side. You make me a better person. There are no words, so I'll stop now.

And to you, my readers, my new friends. Thank you for reading. I hope to meet you all one day over a cup of coffee or a glass of Cabernet and talk shop. Good luck on your journey. I pray for your peace and success. Don't forget to keep your two feet on the ground.

CHAPTER 1

CHOOSE PASSION OVER PAYCHECK

Do you wake up Monday morning and wish it were already Friday? Are you tired of getting a paycheck for doing something you hate? Are you ready to take the plunge into an endless sea of opportunity? Are you prepared to start your own business? If you are, buckle up and get ready for the ride of your life!

We've all heard it, right? "You're starting a business? Make your passion your career!" That's the usual business advice you get when you tell someone you want to start your own business and become an entrepreneur. Sounds incredible! I mean, who wouldn't want to spend their days getting paid for something they love to do?

But the truth is, it's absolutely possible. I am living proof. So is Martha Stewart, as well as many others who have turned their passion into their paycheck. But if there is one key ingredient to your new business venture becoming a success, it's the passion. So before you start, you've got to make sure you LOVE what you're about to do! Think long and hard, and then GET GOING!

#1: You Don't Need Money to Start a Business...You Need Heart

So you're actually going to do it. Congratulations! You will discover along the way that nothing will bring you more self confidence, more gratification, or more financial gain than being your own boss. A bank or a family member could hand you a check for $500,000 to start your own endeavor, but if you don't have the fire, the passion, and the heart as well as the business idea, you might as well throw that check right into a burning fire.

I am a very passionate person, and while my husband sometimes rolls his eyes when I ramble on about some issue that we've gone over a thousand times, my passion has contributed a lot to my success. People gravitate toward passionate people. Think about someone you know who is successful. Don't they make it all seem so easy and effortless? Can't you just see the sparkle in their eyes and feel the fire in their soul? It's infectious.

So before you decide that your destiny is to be an entrepreneur, to be your own boss, you need to have heart. You'll see in this book that you'll need a lot more

than just a prayer, but if you start with
that inner fire, you're halfway there.

#2: Love the Work You Do, and Your Road to Success Will Be a Lot Quicker

"Find a job you *love and you'll never work a day in your life."*—**Confucius**

We've all heard this expression. If you
find something you love to do, it will
never feel like "work." This is true. I'll
never forget how quickly that transition
occurred for me.

When I worked as a Marketing Manager
for a very large electronic components
company, I counted the days, the hours,
the minutes of every week. I used to get
the Sunday afternoon butterflies because
I was never ready to start the workweek.
In fact, Sunday was my least favorite day
of the week. Fridays were like a drug... I
was high all day. But, as soon as I started
my own business, I used to wonder at
how quickly the weeks flew. Working
late into the evenings was exciting for

me, rather than a hindrance. I loved learning new things about my industry, and I loved seeing results. I remember a special product launch one of the world's largest cosmetic companies was doing. We had to come up with a great promo giveaway to pair with one of their shampoos, brand it with their logo, and price it perfectly. I found the item, chiseled the supplier down in price to come in on budget, and then we got the order. It was a tremendous sense of accomplishment. When the work pays off, there's no better feeling. And the thing about owning your own business is that YOU'RE the one who gets to reap the financial benefits of all this creativity and hard work.

So, before taking the plunge, think: "Am I going to love this in 5 years? In 10 years? In 20 years?" I know that may be hard to imagine, but you have to envision yourself doing it day in and day out, for a very long time. If you can't, you haven't unlocked your passion. (See bullet #3!) When you love the work that you do, the days fly by. Think back to your favorite courses in school. Didn't you get your best grades in those courses? The same principle applies to success in your business. If your business excites you, you will work harder, and therefore achieve much greater success.

I have friends who are accountants, and they love it! When they get numbers to balance, it brings them a tremendous sense of satisfaction and accomplishment. If I had to sit behind a computer all day and crunch numbers, I would have to be committed to a loony bin. But that's what makes our lovely world go 'round. One man's (or woman's) meat is another's poison.

#3: Unlock Your Passion

What makes you tick? What is your passion?

I'll never forget how I started my business. I always knew I had an eye for purchasing. For trends. I loved buying gifts for people. So when I finally decided that I wanted to sell gifts for a living, my family looked at me and said, "That's what you want to do with your life? Sell picture frames?" But I knew that I didn't just want to sell one picture frame. I wanted to sell 1,000 picture frames, 100,000 picture frames. I knew that taking my passion, my hobby, and turning it into my career, was the perfect choice for me. My dad said, "With your personality, why don't you consider selling insurance? Insurance salespeople make a lot of money, and it will give you the flexibility in your life you will want down the road as a mother." But my passion for selling insurance was about as strong as my passion for sardines...not very strong.

The other male figure in my life is my wonderful, supportive, and loving husband. I was just 24 years old when I started my promotional products business. Being the impulsive woman that I am, I simply woke up one morning (after deciding that I wanted to go into the corporate gifts business) and QUIT MY JOB. Just like that. My husband was away in New York on a business trip at the time, or so I thought. He called me from New York and asked, "How's your day, honey?"

I answered, "Great, I just quit my job, I'm gonna start my own business after all!" (Another character trait of leading entrepreneurs: they make decisions and stick to them. No one can hold them back or distract them from their vision.)

I couldn't understand why he was stuttering and fumbling on the other line. I hung up disappointed. Why didn't he believe in my dream? Well, the thing I didn't know was that he was there buying my engagement ring, and he was counting on my salary at the time to live on. I was not only giving up my current salary but then was going to have ZERO income for who knew how long? Today we look back and laugh. We were young and naive.

The point in all of this is NO ONE could have talked me out of my decision. All the haters who told me I was entering a competitive marketplace that had no room for me were proven wrong. Moreover, it was the passion that made me never doubt myself. Find yours, unlock it, and in the words of my grandfather, "LET 'ER RIP!"

#4: Don't Do It Just Because It's Cool

Ladies, this isn't high school. You may have tried smoking because it was cool and the "in thing" to do at the time. It was a rite of passage. Coming up with the right business idea is not about what OTHER people are doing. Some may argue this point. Some may say you have to go where the trends are. And I agree that trends are important in creating your product or service. However, I am more of the school of "If you build it, they will come." I truly believe you can CREATE your own trend. You can set the example. You can be the leader instead of the follower.

You may say, "Erica, that is B.S." You may accuse me of starting yet another women's blog. You may think there are millions of blogs already out there, so I did it because it was a trend, or it was "cool." That couldn't be further from the truth. I started my blog with every good intention in the world, yet it was a totally calculated decision as well. It afforded me the luxury of working from home, to be near my kids, and to write and be creative, which I love to do. Through my blog, I could reach out to women around the world and perhaps leave an imprint on their lives. It meant no more managing employees. Although some of you may want to manage employees, I had been there and done that, as they say. I needed more flexibility in my life. And while I may have entered an already crowded area, I wanted it to be a place SPECIFICALLY for women stuck in their lives. I wanted women to feel inspired to create positive change in their lives. While I may be a "Mommy-Blogger," I don't just blog about my life. I like to keep my posts timeless, so that if you stumble upon an old article, it is just as relevant today as it was 3 months ago.

Remember, unlock your passion and do your own thing, on your own terms, with your own vision. Start your business for the right reasons. Don't do it to be cool. Be unique. Be a pioneer. Be a visionary.

#5: What Are You Good At?

If the previous discussion does not seem to connect, let me ask you another question: What are you good at? I mentor a group of businesspeople each month who are looking to either change careers or start their own businesses. As one of the five mentors, we first ask the protégés about their passions and what those are. If they truly cannot make a career out of their passion (as I did, both times), I always ask them, "What are you good at?"

One member of our group has been in Operations for over 25 years. He has worked for large corporations and has completely re-organized their internal corporate structure. He had tremendous success doing this years ago, but the company he recently worked for fell upon hard times, re-structured, and he found himself out of work. So when I met him the first time, and the other mentors asked him, "What's your passion, what do you love to do?" I quietly asked him, "What are you good at?"

Let's face it. This man has a family to support, and he doesn't have the luxury of being out of work for too long. So in deciding if he should become an entrepreneur, which in my opinion, was not the right move for him, I suggested he build on his existing skills, which make him a marketable asset to any corporation. "You should become the 'go-to guy' for operations. Either start your own operations consulting firm, or approach the company you would love to work for and show them everything you've done and why you would be an asset to their company."

So if you are truly gung ho on starting your own business and the passion hasn't come to you, think... What am I good at? What would people be willing to pay for? Your answer may be your next business!

#6: Does It Fit In With Your Life?

As women, we truly are victims of the double standard. While most of our mates (I say most because this doesn't apply to everyone) have the luxury of jetting off to work without a thought about preparing dinner, buying groceries, arranging carpool, extra-curricular activities and so on, we must juggle it all. I will delve into the whole juggling act later, but when you decide where to focus your efforts, the business MUST fit into your life. It must. Period.

For example, I would not recommend that a mom with young children start a restaurant without at least one business partner. We all know the restaurant business runs 24/7, and unless you want your children raised by daycare workers, nannies, or babysitters, it may not be the right time to start this type of business.

As I mentioned before, when I was sitting on the fence in my life not knowing where to channel my energy, the blog fit in perfectly. I was looking to create more of a part-time business, without employees. Go figure! First time around, managing a large staff was all I wanted! But this time, those no longer were my priorities. I didn't want the responsibility of managing employees. I knew a blog would give me the creativity I was looking for, with the potential for a revenue stream from banner advertisements. And look what evolved…a book, as well as numerous other opportunities.

But the point of all of this is that it fit in perfectly with my life and my goals. I wanted to be around for my kids during these formative years, and the blog gave me the flexibility, the enjoyment, and the income potential I was looking for. It fit like a glove. I encourage you to find a business that does the same. As women, we have to look at all aspects of our lives. And our lives are not uni-dimensional. We want fulfilling relationships, time with our children, and personal satisfaction in our own lives. The business has to fit in with those goals. If it doesn't, it won't be successful. You won't have the strength to make it work.

#7: Intend to Leave Your Mark on This World

I love the expression, "Go hard, or go home." I agree whole-heartedly. Anything I have ever done in my life, I have put my all into. I never do anything half-assed. If you are starting a business, you must be ready to play ball. And I say, if you aren't ready to go hard, then STAY HOME!

I think so many women have infinite potential to make incredible changes in this world. There are women making their marks in their own communities and in society that we don't even know about.

It's not just the "Oprahs" that are leaving an imprint on our society. I wrote a blog post about an incredible woman, Terry Grahl, founder of EnchantedMakeovers.org. I encourage you to read her story. She was an award-winning interior decorator who gave up her successful business to make women's shelters a better place to live. She goes from city to city, improving the living conditions for mothers and children, so they live with respect and dignity in a warm environment. This is just one woman of action doing incredible things for our world. Be a woman of action. Go with the intention of creating change. When I get e-mails from women who tell me that they have printed out my tips and posted them on their kitchen bulletin boards as reminders to live the lives they were meant to live, I feel I am making an imprint on their lives. So I encourage you, no matter how small it might be, make your imprint, and don't be fooled. It takes hard work and discipline. And time. But make your mark.

#8: When the Passion Is There, the Money Will Come

Why do we often hear people say, "If you're passionate, you'll be successful at whatever you do?" Because it is true. Let's face it, we're all in business to make money. Money really does make the world go 'round. If you think it doesn't, I think you may be fooling yourself a little. I love those kids who think that all they need is love. Yes, you need love...and a roof over your head, and if you're ambitious, maybe a nice, relaxing vacation every now and then to smooth out the edges. Let's face it, we need money to live. And isn't living comfortably better than slumming it? I certainly think so, and I'm not afraid to say it.

So, when thinking of starting your business, this is why the passion I mentioned previously is so crucial. At the beginning, you may be working 14-hour days. The initial phase of a business start-up requires endless hours of work and

preparation. It's completely exhausting.
So, if it's going to be on your mind 24/7,
you're going to have to be passionate
about it. Then, once it's on your mind
24/7 and things are finally rolling, maybe
wish for a little success!

I love Oprah Winfrey's view on passion,
money and success: "Passion is energy,"
she says. "Feel the power that comes
from focusing on what excites you." Her
show is all about encouraging her
audience to find their passion and live
their dreams. "What I know is, is that if
you do work that you love, and the work
fulfills you, the rest will come," she says.
"And, I truly believe, that the reason I've
been able to be so financially successful
is because my focus has never, ever for
one minute been money."

Well said, O!

#9: Work Hard, But Work Smart!

Hard work => success. Not just hard
work alone...it takes luck, capability,

ambition, and much more to make a business successful, but don't let anyone fool you into thinking that hard work doesn't play a key factor in success. It does! Are you prepared?

I remember, for a fleeting moment, I wanted to open a gift store, instead of selling the corporate route. I thought it would be fun to open up a great-looking retail store, serve lattés to all the clients, and schmooze with them while finding them the perfect gift for their best friend's wedding. My dad, who has always been my greatest protector, told me, "Retail is about the hardest business you could go into. It's not as glamorous as it seems. You're standing on your feet for hours and hours, you can't pull people in off the street, you're left with inventory you can't unload, etc... It's a lot of hard work." Not that I wasn't willing to work hard, but I knew right then and there I had to work SMART. Selling 1 wine decanter was the same effort as selling 1,000 wine decanters.

Which one is more profitable? Catch my drift?

So be prepared to get your hands dirty. It's a long road ahead. There's work to be done! Work hard, but work smart.

CHAPTER 2

BUILD A BUSINESS PLAN TO MAP YOUR TRIP TO SUCCESS

Would you go on a road trip somewhere you've never been without a map (or better yet, a GPS)? Would you go to the grocery store without a list of things you need? If you have ever gone to the grocery store without a list, no doubt when you got home you remembered several things you meant to get but simply forgot. Your business will work the same way. Your business plan is probably the single most important document you will create in your venture. The #1 reason businesses fail is because of a lack of planning.

This section is not a "step-by-step" action plan to create a business plan from A to Z. You can go to the bank, get an application form, and ask people to guide you through that process. This chapter gives you something better. It gives you the "ins and outs" to actually getting it approved! This is the-behind-the scenes work needed to make it sizzle and to make sure your business plan sells itself. You must have a stellar business plan. No shortcuts.

#10: Think Girl Scouts: "Be Prepared."

Nothing feels better than being your own boss, making your own decisions, calling the shots, and turning your dream into a reality. But to make all of this possible, you need one special ingredient. Preparedness. You have to think like a Girl Scout, and always be prepared. I can't stress enough how the word P-R-E-P-A-R-E-D takes on so many different meanings when you become an entrepreneur.

- Be prepared in your business plan, which is your roadmap to success.
- Be prepared for mistakes to happen *often* in the beginning, and be ready with a solution when that happens.
- Be prepared to work hard, as I mentioned previously.
- Be prepared to be disappointed along the way, or better yet, surprisingly delighted.
- BE PREPARED FOR ANYTHING WHEN YOU START YOUR OWN BUSINESS!

#11: Developing the Realistic Business Plan

If there is one word of advice I could give you ladies, it's to make sure your business plan is realistic. When I prepared my business plan for the bank, it looked great on paper. All the I's were dotted, all the T's were crossed...at first glance. However, I generously expected my gross profits (GP) to be 40% consistently, so if I was forecasting $1,000,000 a year in sales, I assumed $400,000 was gross profit. Wow! Was I in for a hard dose of reality!

Besides my mistake in forecasting that not every year was a 40% GP year, my overhead ended up being way higher than I'd planned for as well. Every little thing adds up, and you shouldn't be fooled. Yes, your business plan is your masterpiece to show to an investor to get start-up capital, but it is YOUR GUIDE as well. Make it realistic. There is nothing more disappointing than coming off a bad year.

Another thing to contemplate when making a realistic budget: are you pricing your goods and services high enough? Many start-ups undervalue their offer, and as a result, end up making less money. Many start-ups also don't know their fixed and variable costs, their average sale, their break-even point (see point #26), their frequency of leads or customer visits, and the list goes on and on. The first few years are very heavy.

So I urge you, give your business plan the time it needs. Often, as leaders and self-starters, we make the mistake of being overly anxious and rushing through the business plan just to "get it done." I can't stress enough: take your time and do the research, which leads us into our next point.

#12: The No-Brainer— Industry/Market Research

You wouldn't leave for a road trip in the winter without checking road conditions. Similarly, you shouldn't start a business without checking the market conditions. Industries change over the years. What you think about one industry may not apply anymore.

When I started my premium and incentive business, I didn't do nearly enough market research. I knew it was a saturated market with a lot of competition, and that didn't scare me. What I failed to learn was that margins weren't what they once were. In a perfect world, those margins should have been 40% to 50%. But no one told me that in order to get the lucrative contracts, you had to practically give it away for free! Our industry margins were becoming totally eroded. People were setting up shop in their basements with a catalog and a business card, with little overhead, and off they went chasing the big business. Those of us with the big overhead of staff and office space were behind the eight ball. This was happening to our industry, and I wasn't prepared for it.

So get to the library! Go to your competition. Talk to people. Use the Internet to do your research. You have to know the ins and outs of your industry cold. This is all part of preparing the best business plan possible. Be prepared for those roadblocks no one told me about.

#13: What's Your Edge? Chances Are You'll Need Some Funding!

Remember economics? We all learned a term: USP (Unique Selling Proposition). What are you selling that is so unique? What's your edge? This is crucial knowledge for your bank, and it's crucial knowledge for you as well. Unless you've saved up a ton of money, you are a trust fund baby, or have a wealthy husband, you're going to need a line of credit. Someone has to believe in you to take a chance on you. If you have no edge, if you come on like just another fish in the sea, good luck getting that start-up capital.

Your business plan should also be tailored to who is going to be reading it. Your audience will shape it. For example, are you going to venture capitalists or a bank for the money? A business plan for investors is typically 15 to 30 pages in length, whereas one for a bank is typically 10 to 15 pages in length. Investors want to see potential return on investment (i.e., a chance to make some money with your business), whereas a bank just wants to make sure its loan is repaid.

That being said, you need to have an edge to lure in the money guys. When I started my promotional business, I didn't want to be just another person with a catalog. I called my company Unique Corporate Gifts. First, I wanted the word UNIQUE to be there. People love uniqueness. Secondly, I decided I was going to be the "go-to" person for everything corporate gift-related. So I wasn't just going to sell you caps, pens, and mugs with your logo. I was going to get your best customers front-row seats to the best sporting events and a signed Michael Jordan jersey for your other great client. My angle was one-stop-shopping for all corporate needs. And it worked.

#14: The Biggest Expense—Your Employees!

Aah, the question about the people. How many? What should you pay them? After all, it's all about the people, ain't it? And I have to tell you…it is!

A word of advice: when hiring employees, it's a good idea to search for people whose traits complement your strengths and weaknesses. What's the point of hiring 10 of yourself? When a bunch of different people with diverse traits and talents come together to the drawing board, the output you get is 100 times more creative!

The one thing I found most challenging about starting my business was finding good people at the salary that most start-ups usually can afford…minimal! I was also a control freak (big mistake) and liked the way **I** did things. I always found myself frustrated with the level of competency of my employees in the early years, and truly, I was to blame. But the truth is, YOU GET WHAT YOU PAY FOR. You may be like me and think you can do it all yourself. But I promise you, you cannot.

So make sure you budget for good people. I will expand more on the importance of good employees in bullet point #20. It may be only one part-time person at the beginning, but don't try and do it all yourself. Trying to do everything yourself goes against point #9 about working smart. Have those capable people built into your business plan. Great employees can act as sounding boards and bring a tremendous amount of knowledge to the table. Even if your business is small, this rule still applies. If there is anything I can't stress enough, it's this—don't skimp on your people! Then refer to your market research to know what a good salesperson, controller, or assistant would demand as a salary in your field. Be prepared!

#15: Think Organic

I'm a believer in karma. I also believe that things happen the way they need to happen, and we must never ignore the message. Even with the male-dominated left side of my brain always working, I am still spiritual and holistic in my thoughts. I believe that businesses have the greatest success when they're grown organically. But don't be fooled: organic growth still requires that you create your business with intention and careful planning.

When you think "Organic," you probably think of fruits, vegetables, baby food, and now even wine! Many things are labeled "organic" today. When people think of organic growth, they think of things happening naturally, almost effortlessly. In terms of my blog, growing it organically means that Search Engine Optimization (SEO) will be cheaper and more effective long term than a pay-per-click program. In organic growth, it takes longer to see results, but the results are usually more effective and long lasting. I suppose "natural growth" is not something you would associate with business, but that couldn't be further from the truth.

So, what is organic growth? Well, in the business sense, it means growing your business without any mergers, acquisitions, or takeovers. It is the rate at which a company grows by using its own resources to grow its sales. Some say organic growth is a good indicator of how well management has used its own resources to expand.

At the start-up phase, deciding whether to grow organically depends on your business type. If you are a start-up that is going to require a tremendous amount of investment capital, organic growth may not be possible, and your control over the company may be limited as well. However, your growth may be quicker. If you choose to grow organically, you will probably grow slower but maintain greater control over your company and its vision. However, there is a greater risk of a competitor getting ahead of you.

These are issues to contemplate when starting your business. These choices of direction must be carefully mapped out in your plan.

#16: Put Yourself Into the Business Plan. Think Personality.

No one ever tells you to do this. This is never one of the steps in "Business Plan Writing 101." But it is a key factor that will make investors more keen at throwing money your way.

If I asked you 10 great attributes about yourself, what would they be? This is the "sell yourself" part of the business plan. (I'll discuss more in- depth later). You are the driving force behind the idea. Banks don't invest in companies: they invest in the PEOPLE creating and driving the companies, so make sure all your best attributes are in that business plan. Don't hold back!!

One of the reasons my bank gave me a line of credit of almost $100,000 in the blink of an eye when I was 24 years old is because they believed in ME as the driving force of the company. I showed them my sales action plan. I told them about the sales awards I had won and proved to them that my selling skills were my talent. Because I was a distributor with little overhead and no machinery (I was just the middleman), my business model was very sales-driven. I made them feel comfortable taking a chance on me. It's all about <u>you</u> as the creator.

Never forget to put <u>yourself</u> in that business plan.

#17: Presenting Your Plan to the Bank — How to Get Them to Buy Into the Dream

You want your investors to think that they have the next Microsoft on their hands. Well, maybe not Microsoft, but certainly a profitable money-making machine. I don't have to tell you that it has to be typewritten, properly edited, and professional looking.

Keep in mind that your business plan will set the tone for how your business will operate in reality, so it shouldn't have a bunch of jargon and irrelevant information in it. Think of it as like handing in a pilot for a TV series. It has to captivate the readers right away. You need them to buy into the dream— LITERALLY!

Remember, the presentation of your business plan is YOUR TIME TO SHINE. This is it! Walk in confident but humble. You are starting this business because you believe in it. Make them believe in it too. I always liked to let the bank know that I needed them, but not too much. If I didn't get what I wanted from them, I could walk to the bank next door. The relationship between you and your investors is a business relationship. Don't ever forget that.

#18: Your Planning Doesn't Stop With the Written Final Business Plan

Okay, you've submitted your business plan, and it's approved! Whoo hoo! Break open the bubbly! You must celebrate every milestone. However, there's one big BUT. *This is only the beginning.* Now is when your business plan really starts to evolve.

The minute that plan gets approved, you will never stop planning. Over time, your business plan will need to be adjusted, re-written, and re-tweaked. Your business and its needs will change along the way, and your plan will have to reflect those changes. Part of being an entrepreneur is being adaptable and accepting change.

This isn't always easy, and it takes us out of our comfort zone, but if you're paralyzed by change, you may not have the stomach for this thing we call "becoming your own boss."

CHAPTER 3

THINK BIG, START SMALL

If you don't start small, you will never start at all. Starting a business has truly become one of the American Dreams. It can give you financial freedom, freedom to call the shots, and freedom to go at your own pace. For me, I would never have had it any other way. Entrepreneurship is not for everyone. It is not for the weak in the knees or those with a queasy stomach. At times, it can truly be an out-of-body experience.

But you've decided to do it, so why not make it the best it can be? Why not aim for the stars? But before you go quitting your day job, you can still plan the dream and move with caution. In fact, most successful businesses today, such as Microsoft, started with this motto, "Think Big, Start Small." There is a tremendous amount of commitment required to make it successful, and there is no shame in starting small.

So think gardening, ladies. Think of some of the most beautiful trees or flowers you've planted. The earth is laid, the seed is planted, and with the right amount of light and water, slowly, you start to grow a big, beautiful plant. Your business needs the same kind of nurturing. Plant the seed, give it the love and attention it needs, and slowly watch it grow.

#19: Don't Quit Your Day Job Just Yet, Oprah!

Although it's very possible you are the next Oprah Winfrey, don't quit your day job just yet. It's possible to do both until your new venture is off the ground. I made this mistake when I started my business, but I was in a financially stable position and could make that mistake. I was 24 and still living at home. (That was a whole other story, don't laugh!) But my point is, I was making about $40,000 a year and saving practically every dollar I earned. I was impulsive, and I believed in my idea so strongly that I didn't think twice about writing a business plan, walking into the bank, getting a line of credit, quitting my day job, and calling everyone I knew to get them to buy my corporate gifts.

But for most people who are not in a position to go for extended periods of time without a steady income, definitely do not quit your day job prematurely. I know this can be quite difficult. You come home exhausted at the end of the day, and then you only have nights and weekends to work on your new business. So it becomes a bit of a catch-22. You can't grow your business without fully dedicating your time, and you can't fully dedicate your time until it's finally growing. But it is possible.

Another good reason not to quit your job too quickly is that by still having that full-time job, there is no pressure to make your venture happen too quickly. You're able to make some mistakes along the way, and it won't mean the end of the world.

Try to find the balance between working two jobs, and hopefully it won't be long before you're up and running, and deriving some revenue from your new business. Then you can hand in your 2 weeks and go hard, 24/7!

#20: You've Got to Spend to Make!

George Steinbrenner, the famous name behind the legendary New York Yankees, had a winning strategy. He had a strict policy dictating how he assembled the team: Hire the best at any cost. He had no problem paying huge prices for players he knew would help the team win the World Series. He knew there was nothing as valuable as having the best people. He called it "Winning at any cost." He hired the best management as well. So he paid the best, but he also expected the best.

When I was running my business, I was nowhere near the size of the New York Yankees, but I ran it with the same policy…just with many less ZEROES! I rewarded good employees, I paid extra for an attractive website, I created a showroom with nice lighting and a soft look, and I filled it with great-looking samples. I always got three quotes for everything I bought, and I spent with caution. But I invested in my company. When looking at the company's best interests, I knew my time was best spent selling. But as I was growing, I was still trying to manage sales, accounting, orders, etc. I realized this was no way to grow. I hired an amazing assistant. Her salary ate away at my bottom line, but the benefits were far greater than the alternative. It allowed me to grow! And from there, I never hesitated to spend if it was for the purpose of improving productivity.

Another great example is my blog. I started it as a creative outlet and a hobby, so I used a standard free blogging platform when I set it up. However, I didn't love the look of the site, so I spent a little money updating it. I tried to cut corners and save costs, and in the end, got a product that had glitches and was flawed. I am in the process of having to spend major dollars to have it redone to rectify all the issues, so in the end, it has cost me even more. Had I done it right the first time around, I would have saved the time, energy, and expense. Catch my drift?

#21: Dress for Success

You have to learn how to play the game. I'll let you in on a little secret—everyone loves to be associated with a winner. People love to surround themselves with the best. On the days that I was featured in the press, either on television or in the newspaper; I would get TONS of new calls for new business. People gravitate towards leaders. It's such an overused concept in business, but it has weight.

Unfortunately, we live in a shallow world. After all, you want to feel confident with the person you are buying ANYTHING from. Confidence is a very powerful thing in sales. If you LOOK the part, you BECOME the part, at least in the eyes of your customers.

Now, I will tell you, there is a fine line between looking powerful and confident, and overdoing it. This is always a source of debate. You don't want to look TOO successful, causing your clients to believe you're making **too much** money, but then you want them to think you are a player in your industry. Ah, the fine balance. But I still think you can dress for success without overdoing it. Look the part. With some luck and hard work, you WILL become the part!

#22: Start Your Community Work Early

This is a perfect place to discuss the art of giving. You need to give back to your community early in your business start-up. Everyone needs to get involved in something, both personally and professionally. We are not on this earth to suck up everything we can get our hands on. Even if it isn't much, you must be a giver. Communities like to support those that give back. When I look at my community, the ones who are successful are also big givers. Yes, it's true; they give a lot because they can afford to give. Nevertheless, many of these companies were giving long before they became financially solid.

The day I opened I business, before I had $1 in sales, I made a pledge to give a percentage of my yearly net sales to various breast cancer research causes. Breast cancer was a cause very close to my heart because my family had been touched by the illness. It made me very proud to be able to give back. Obviously, it wasn't much during the first few years, but it was a commitment, and every dollar counts. And it felt great. I also gave more than just money, I gave of my TIME. I volunteered at the emergency department at the local hospital. I served meals for people living below the poverty line and much, much more.

Once again, people not only like to buy from winners, they like to buy from givers. Give what you can, right from the start.

#23: Starting Small Is the Best Way to Get You on Your Way

Ladies, there's nothing wrong with starting small. Don't let anyone tell you otherwise. You can still look the part, act the part, think big, but start small. I follow an entrepreneur who sold her business for £50,000,000, and she now coaches and mentors entrepreneurs as a way to give back. She says she can always spot a winning entrepreneur when she sees one. She claims that while many of them can analyze complex stats, most are paralyzed when it comes to getting their businesses off the ground. The most successful entrepreneurs she has seen started small.

So why start small? One reason is to overcome the overwhelming sense of responsibility that comes with starting your own business. I remember moving full steam ahead with my business, and then 3 months into the process, I woke up one morning PANICKED. "Holy cow," I thought, "if this thing doesn't work out, I am liable for $100,000." I totally freaked out. I felt completely overwhelmed and realized right then and there the huge undertaking I had just embarked on. For this reason, I urge you to start small.

By starting small you will also be able to control your growth and prioritize your goals. It keeps your life and your business manageable. I have worked with many entrepreneurs over the years, and

it's the steady ones who are still around.
Think big, start small.

#24: Giving 1% Extra Effort a Day

I decided to put this in the book because
one of my blog posts covered this topic,
and I think it is a powerful concept. A
rabbi said many years ago that by giving
an extra 1% of daily effort, we can self-
improve 365% by year's end! It may
seem like a rather ridiculous
pronouncement, but I realized, as I have
grown and learned, that his words ring
true.

Giving an extra 1% of ourselves seems
easy. But the point in all of this is that
starting small leads to big change. So live
by the words of the rabbi. Aim for small
changes, and you will see great things
happen. Give the extra 1% to all facets of
your life—your marriage, your children,
your community, your business. It's only
a little bit of extra effort each day
distributed amongst all these areas, but

by going the extra distance, you will see great changes.

Think of it this way; if you succeed in giving only an extra 1% a day, for a third of the year, you will still be approximately 100% better off. (If you're not good at math, 1/3 of 365 is approximately 100!) Think of splitting that 100% between all the things that matter to you. All of a sudden, you are a better spouse, mother, friend, and businesswoman. You will then be setting an example for those around you. Your employees will follow as well. By giving more, you end up getting more, and for me...nothing could be better or more rewarding!

#25: Start From Home. Are You Sure You Need That Corner Office Right Away?

This was a great help to me financially. I started my business from our home office. The lower you can keep your overhead, the more money you'll make, right? And this pertains not only to the start-up phase either. This matters throughout the life of your business. Only when the gifts were taking over our basement then the entire house did I get a SMALL office. Key word: small. I never took on more than I could handle financially. And, it doesn't mean that when I did finally take on that small office space, I didn't decorate it beautifully with fresh-cut flowers, paintings, and plants. However, I budgeted. As the saying goes, I cut the cloth according to the measure. This is huge.

But, when I eventually moved a second time and got the big corner office, it was because we were truly busting out of our other place. There is nothing wrong with spending to increase productivity, or to truly enhance your business. But do you need that office just yet? Can you not start from home? When you work from home, you don't waste resources. Think about it before committing to a space.

#26: Don't Panic When You See the First Year's Earnings!

In your business plan, there should be a "Break-Even Analysis" section. You MUST know what that magic number is. Your break-even point is the amount of revenue you need to bring in to cover your expenses before you make a dime of profit. Obviously, if your revenues are higher than your expenses in the first year, that's very encouraging. That's what we call profit, my friends, and that's a great thing! Celebrate the milestone.

But don't panic either if you haven't yet turned a profit. Every business is different, and there is no rule of thumb for when you will turn a profit. For some businesses it happens very quickly, and for others it can take a few years before you see a return on your investment. Check your business plan. See if you came close to what you had forecasted. What went right, and what went wrong? And remember, be patient. It is by no means reason to throw in the towel if you haven't turned a profit in year one.

#27: Every Big-Time CEO Has a Mentor. Why Shouldn't You?

Every entrepreneur, no matter how big or small, needs a mentor. There is a lot to be learned from the successful people who have walked life before you. You hear it every day. Maya Angelou is rumored to have mentored Oprah, Ray Charles mentored Quincy Jones, Sidney Poitier mentored Denzel Washington, and so on.

A mentor is a positive role model in a person's life, and it goes way beyond just business. Mentors have been proven to help shape today's youth and keep them on the right path (a great example is Big Brothers, Big Sisters Organization). The benefits are astonishing. So find yourself a business mentor early in the start-up process. He or she will be your confidante, your guide, your sounding board, and your "go-to" person when the going gets tough. Sometimes we need a person removed from our inner circle to shed light on a situation—someone objective and knowledgeable in our field.

Going online is a great place to start to find a mentor. He or she will be the guiding force, a member of your board of directors, and your teacher. Every entrepreneur should have one.

CHAPTER 4

IT'S ALL IN THE ATTITUDE

Question: What key attributes do most successful business owners and entrepreneurs possess?

Answer: Talent, skill, and drive.

Many other people already doing what you are about to do possess these attributes as well. You're probably not the first talented and driven person to start a business in your field. So what will set you apart from your competition?

What will be one of the major deciding
factors in your success? I know it sounds
simplistic, but it's all in the attitude,
baby! Your mental toughness, your
emotional strength, your attitude, your
will, and your positive mental state will
drive your success. This holds true far
beyond just the business arena. Consider
Michael Jordan and Roger Federer;
besides having tremendous talent on the
basketball and tennis courts, these men
possess an extreme mental toughness and
incredible fighting attitude. They never
give up on themselves. Attitude plays a
key role in success. Don't let anyone ever
tell you otherwise.

#28: Believe in Yourself

For some people, believing in themselves
is easy. Some women are blessed with
incredible self-esteem and tremendous
confidence. For these women, self-doubt
is just not something they experience
often; they are goal-oriented and
extremely focused. For other women,
believing in themselves doesn't come as

easily and naturally. But let me tell you, ladies, believing in yourself is the first step to success. If you lack confidence, it will be difficult to succeed in anything, let alone in your new business.

I assume if you have decided to start your own business, you are probably a natural born leader, a risk taker, or assertive. All of these qualities are character traits of self-starters. So, no doubt you already have some degree of belief in yourself and the journey you are embarking upon. This self-belief is excellent, because the most successful business owners believe so strongly in what they're doing and in the message they are spreading.

So try to set yourself up for success, *not failure.* As you swim along the stream of life, make your goals and expectations realistic. Achieving your goals raises your confidence level. When you keep these goals realistic, you make them manageable, which allows even the toughest critics (ourselves) to believe. One final word of advice on believing in yourself: listen to the "haters", because they often have good constructive criticism, but don't give them the power to make you believe that you're "less than." Don't let them get you down. I never let the haters get me down. They may have knocked me down a few times, but they never *kept* me down. They're there to keep us grounded, to keep things real, and to teach us where we can improve. That's about it.

#29: The Art of Positive Thinking

"I think, therefore I am." —Rene Descartes

There is no better life than a positive and happy life. Positive thinking is crucial to your long-term success in both life and business. If only life was as easy as Barbara Eden's on "I Dream of Jeannie." We could just blink our eyes, and all would be sunny. If only... Positive thinking is easier said than done, but most successful business leaders I know are tremendously positive. There is no half-empty glass...it's ALWAYS full. Successful people believe that the universe will support them no matter what. I have always prided myself on being a positive-thinking person. I am known to get easily stressed and sometimes panic too soon, but my overall attitude is positive and optimistic. This positive outlook has helped me overcome many business hardships.

So how do you become a positive thinker, so that you think, therefore you are? Here are a few things you can do:

- Be aware of your thoughts. Once you develop a heightened sense of awareness of your negative thoughts, you can focus on them and begin to make changes.
- Do what I often do, and what you've already done—look for self-help guides. There are so many great ones available that give you valuable tips and techniques on how to stay positive, even during tough times.

I love self-help guides. I place them on my night table, so that when I'm feeling vulnerable, I open them up and get re-juiced!

- Be thankful for what you do have, and for what is good in your life. We've become such an overachieving society, and we are constantly bombarded with images of success on the news. We've lost sight of the fragility of life. We have become greedy, and we're not nearly thankful enough. So even when times are tough, appreciate what you DO have, and don't lose sight of that.

#30: Do What Oprah Says... Make a Vision Board!

The Vision Board episode that changed my life aired on March 14, 2008. Oprah was discussing the Laws of Attraction and the book *The Secret* with author Rhonda Byrne. A vision board is a dream board or goal board. It contains every hope and aspiration for success. It seemed like a dumb idea at first, but something clicked for me. I have a Bristol board of homemade cuttings and clippings that represents my entire PLAN. Family, kids, business, success, music, happiness, peace, gardening, yoga, and of course, ME SITTING ON OPRAH'S COUCH!

I encourage all of you ladies to make a vision board. The board will cost you mere peanuts, and it will enable you to begin creating a montage of what you want your life to look like. It should be in a visible place, so you never take your eye off the prize. Maybe for you, it's to become a Fortune 500 Company. Post that logo up there, baby! Maybe it's to juggle your business and family with ease—let that be represented on your vision board as well. Whether it's a personal dream or professional goal, it should all be there. It goes back to the previous quote by Rene Descartes, "I think, therefore I am."

#31: Never Take "No" For An Answer...

It's called tenacity. One of the key factors in the success of your business is your ability to not take "No" for an answer and to be persistent. I was famous in my industry for my relentless persistence. My suppliers sensed me coming from a mile away! I think I even irritated them quite a bit with how hard I pushed them. If a client needed an order in 3 days, you better believe I would find a supplier who could give me a quality job in 3 days. You have to learn to be resourceful in business, and part of that is not accepting "No" too easily.

I remember my husband used to say to me, "You're driving your suppliers crazy!" I didn't care. I was good to them. I was very loyal to them. In return, I expected a partnership. In fact, it used to irritate me when people said "No" right away. I would often be in the middle of a sentence, and I would hear, "No, we can't produce an order in 5 days. We rely on our button supplier, and he can't ship before 9 days." As persistent as I am, I would try and think FOR the other person. My answer would be something like, "If *I* find you a button supplier who can ship you the buttons for tomorrow, can I have my order in 5 days?"

Do you see where I'm going with this? Help them to help you get what you want and need. Remember one of Tom Cruise's famous lines in the movie *Jerry Maguire*? "Help me, help you." The same applies in business.

And this doesn't apply just to your suppliers, obviously. Don't let your salespeople say they can't do something, or let them give up too easily either. Guide them and help THEM to achieve. Don't let ANYONE say "No" to you unless it's physically impossible. You move mountains for your customers. Allow others to move mountains for you, too. This is your success on the line. Which then leads to point #32...

#32: But Then Again, Don't Beat a Dead Horse

Alright, here we go again: the fine balance. I've just finished telling you never to take "No" for an answer, and to push, push, push. However, ladies, don't beat a dead horse! If you've tried all the avenues to make something happen to no avail, sometimes you'll just have to take that no, bite the bullet, and wish for better luck next time. Sometimes we have to take our losses and move on without grinding out a situation and wasting our time.

So how do you know when to push and when to surrender? This is tricky. I'll tell you that it does come with time and experience. If something seems completely impossible, no matter how persistent you are, chances are it's probably truly impossible. So, you may really want an order desperately, but if the client is truly asking for the impossible, you will have to say the forbidden word... "No." Forget it, pull yourself up by your bootstraps, and move on! Plain and simple. It's all in the attitude, remember?

#33: Personal Responsibility—The "Must-Have" Attitude in Business

We're gonna do a little Psych 101 here. After all, I am a psych major. If there is any character trait that I most dislike in people, it's when they blame the world for their problems and feel that they have no control over their lives. They refuse to take responsibility for their actions. To me, this is a bad attitude to adopt, and not the right way to approach your life. Things like: "I can't," or "It wasn't my fault," or "She started it." This may very well be true, but most of the time, it's not. In fact, you see it often with depression or alcoholism, for example. Yes, it's true, we may have predispositions to certain illnesses or character traits, but you do have control over your destiny and how you choose to handle those pre-dispositions. Saying "I'm depressed because my parents were depressed" places the blame on **someone else,** and zero responsibility on you. In turn, you simply surrender the chance for anything good to happen in your life.

This principle applies in business, just as in life. As the leader of your company, you must also take responsibility for your shortcomings in your own journey. If sales are weak, you can't just blame the economy or your salespeople. You have to take a deeper look at what's going on. Perhaps you didn't push as hard as you could have. There's a certain amount of responsibility that we are often afraid to take upon ourselves. Ladies, it's not a dark place to be. It's an honest place. And 9 times out of 10, you end up learning a valuable lesson along the way when you take personal responsibility for your shortcomings.

#34: Successful People See the Glass as Half Full

Think of Tony Robbins. It can get annoying after a while...all that positive energy. You wonder if it's real or not, I must admit. I once asked a successful entrepreneur how he stays so positive during the rough patches and dark moments. He replied, "Erica, every day I have a choice. I wake up, and I can choose to be happy, and in a good mood, or I can choose to be pissed off and in a crappy mood. I figure there's no point in the latter." And something in what he said resonated with me. I realized attitude is a CHOICE. It's something we choose, and I choose to be positive. It's as simple as that.

When I started my business, no matter how bad my day was, no matter how frazzled I felt or how big the order that I lost was, I still saw my glass as half full. I mourned the loss, and then I moved on. I tried not to dwell in the past or stay stuck for too long. Then I tried to learn from those bad moments or mistakes and once again, never ignore the message.

#35: Spread the Good Feeling to Your Employees—It Has to Come from the Top

I cannot stress the importance of this point enough. NO matter what kind of day I was having, I never tried to lose my game face. You just have to keep it on for the sake of your employees. Some may disagree, but I really feel strongly about this. There is a line. You are the boss; your employees work for you. That means they take their cues and direction from you. Have you ever worked at a company where the owners were negative, verbally abusive, and pessimistic? Have you ever worked for the boss from hell? How did you feel? What was the corporate morale like? Don't ever make that mistake. Remember, you are the ringleader, and your team members will follow your cue. Set a good example right from the start.

To connect with my team, I used to meet with them EVERY Monday morning at 9 AM. I used to kick the week off with fresh coffee and donuts. We used to shoot the breeze; how was everyone's weekend, how were the kids, the husband, the boyfriend, the knitting project, whatever. I got to know about each and every employee's life, their children, their dogs, their mistresses...just kidding! We used to sit down as a company, and discuss the things we were succeeding at, and the areas that needed improvement. I encouraged everyone to participate and voice their opinion. I approached the meeting with a smile and a helpful attitude. If you show your employees the image and energy level that you as a company want to portray to your clients, they will catch on. In a way, employees are like children: you must watch *what you say* and *how you act* when you're in front of them. You are their role model, and they will copy you.

#36: Failure Is Not an Option

Don't you feel like you're listening to a pep talk right before a football game? This is something I can picture a coach shouting at his team: "Go out and play your hardest. Failure is not an option." Now this may be a strong statement to make and one that I always try to live by, but in actuality, some of your businesses may just not make it. Hopefully, you'll all soar to new heights, and maybe thank me one day for the tips, but there is that small chance of failure. Despite this chance, get failure out of your head. Come on, stand up now, and shake the "*failies*" out—if that's a word!?!?!

I'll never forget my summer camp experiences in my early years. I learned a valuable lesson from my father. Being the pretty good salesperson that I am, I convinced them to let me go to sleep-away camp at 8 years old (even though they questioned whether I was too young). I told them "Yes, I am ready," and I proceeded to name all the reasons why sleep-away camp was the perfect thing for me. Well, day 1 and day 2 were fantastic. Day 3, I woke up crying hysterically and missing my parents beyond comprehension. I convinced the camp owner to let me call them. "I want to come home. Please pick me up," I cried on the phone to Mom and Dad.

My father picked up the phone after I had cried to my mother for 12 minutes. He said quietly and calmly, "This was your choice. You made a commitment, and you will see it through. We are not picking you up. Stay there, enjoy camp, and make the best out of the rest of your time. Sweetie, you are not a quitter. I love you, and don't call back!" Can you believe that??? But for him, quitting or failing was not an option. There's always that chance of failure when you start a business, but you've got to keep it in the far distance emotionally. And NO, ladies, failure will not be your option either!

CHAPTER 5

KNOW HOW TO SELL YOURSELF

The art of self promotion is an essential skill for the self-employed. It's not the product or service people are buying, it's YOU! In business, image is everything. If you are reading this guide, then you probably already possess the traits of a leader. Leaders must know how to sell themselves. Your ability to show your best qualities can be a crucial factor in signing business deals, increasing sales, and luring in the best employees. Think about it this way: if you cannot sell yourself as a person to others, how do you think you are going to be able to sell your goods and services? This skill does not come easily to everyone. Not everyone has perfected the art of "self-promotion." But it can be done, and it MUST be done to convince ANYONE to take a chance on you. Read on, ladies...

#37: If You Can't Sell Yourself, You Ain't Gonna Sell Anything!

If I told you that you had 1 minute to sell yourself, would you know how to do it? If you had to create your own infomercial, would you know what to cover? Now stay with me, and don't cringe with stage fright. We haven't all mastered the art of self-promotion as effortlessly as Donald Trump, but it is a staple for the success of your business. So, get out of your head that being a self-promoter is a bad thing and perfect your infomercial.

The art of convincing someone else that you are best suited for the job is crucial.

And I'm not just talking about a job interview. I'm talking about selling yourself to your potential clients, because at the end of the day, that's what they are buying... YOU. Obviously your product or service must be of superior quality; that goes without saying. But you need to make your clients comfortable placing their trust in you, all while appearing genuine and authentic. It takes practice.

So before you pick up the phone to call a new prospect or walk into a meeting to pitch your product or service, think confidence. SPEAK CONFIDENTLY. Watch your tone and your body language. If you come prepared, you will know your stuff cold, which will in turn bring you the confidence you need to help sell yourself. So remember, preparedness is a key factor in the ability to sell YOU. Always be prepared!

#38: Gotta Love 7 AM Networking Breakfasts! Quick, Tell Me About Yourself!

Part of getting a business off the ground is being EVERYWHERE. This is a crucial aspect to growing a young business, and is discussed not nearly enough. When I started my business, right until the day I sold it, I WAS OUT THERE. I joined the local Chamber of Commerce, I attended networking events, conferences, and seminars. You name it, I was there. "Oh, there's that girl Erica again," I'm sure people thought. But don't be fooled; it's necessary. I don't care if you've decided to become a massage therapist, a lawyer, or an Internet marketer: anyone trying to sell anything needs to be out there.

Those 7 AM networking breakfasts brought me a lot of early success. My alarm would go off, and I would say to myself almost every time, "I'm skipping this one. I don't feel like going this morning," but I always left the breakfast with one new lead. And one new lead led to the next new lead...and on and on it rolled. Don't skip the 7 AM breakfasts. They eventually pay off.

#39: Learn How to Listen—Quiet Confidence Speaks Loudly

I have two words for you... Bill Gates. This guy is one of the most powerful men in the world. Contrary to Donald Trump, he can enter and exit a room without being heard much; however, he cannot enter or leave a room without being FELT. His quiet confidence is palpable. While this style may be different than the overt personality type, there is something stellar about a quiet presence. And the art of listening is an acquired skill. It comes with a certain level of achievement, although not always. It is one of my weaknesses that I constantly work on.

I know an exceptionally successful billionaire entrepreneur. When I was running my company, I loved to talk to him. Contrary to other successful business people I had been around, this guy didn't talk a lot. He was an incredible listener. He used to ask ME all the questions. It was like he wanted to learn from every person he came into contact with. He just soaked up knowledge, and he was an *active listener*; he didn't just wait his turn to speak. He was genuinely listening to and learning from the world. I learned a lot from that style. I agree it may not be mine (I'm outgoing to a fault), but learn how to listen. That quiet confidence also sells. Try to figure out what style works best for you then work it to your advantage. By learning to listen more, you will learn more about your prospect, and you'll be better equipped to satisfy their needs. God gave us two ears and only one mouth. There's your cue.

#40: If You're Unique, Selling Yourself and Your Product Will Come a Lot More Easily

Think Unique! And see lucky tip #13! What makes you so special? What's your edge? Have you taken the ordinary and created it with a twist? If so, you will undoubtedly have people eating out of your hand. If you build it, they will come. But don't be discouraged if you haven't uncovered that uniqueness just yet. There are lots of subtle ways that you can take the ordinary and make it extraordinary. Perhaps you're able to do the same job as your competition, only faster. Maybe the vision comes to you with great ease, thereby turning your product or service around quicker than the average. These are strengths. Play to these strengths. Or maybe you are opening a retail store. Why not give everyone who purchases a certain dollar amount of merchandise or greater a set of movie tickets? These are little things you can do to make your product or service more attractive to the buyer.

The point in all of this is figure out why you are unique. When you uncover your uniqueness, you will be confident about what you're selling, and that confidence becomes infectious. People will believe in you and your product, and that can only convert to dollar signs.

#41: We're All Born Salespeople! (Does Your Kid Ever Twist Your Arm into That Second Bowl of Ice Cream?)

If you think you're not a born salesperson, think again. We're all salespeople! Even your kid is a salesperson. Do you ever find yourself giving in to your child when they ask to stay up that extra hour at night? They're selling you. Don't think for 1 minute that this isn't selling! If you think you're more the "artsy" type and not a "born" salesperson, I'm telling you, you are! If you think you're best suited behind the desk, instead of in front of it, then think again. I have news for you: even if you are starting an accounting firm and think that you may be the "typical" accountant, you will still need dynamic selling skills.

So, how can you become a salesperson in any business?

- First, remember, you are an inborn, natural selling type already. Play on it. One of the women I mentor on a monthly basis has an incredible business idea, but she is so unsure of herself that she doubts the whole project and its success. I made her realize that not everyone's selling type is the Trump type. I encourage her to stay focused on improving her incredible idea. When she talks about her product, her passion is palpable, even through her shyness. That genuine quality IS her selling talent. She may not be the aggressive type, but she is just as believable because of her authentic style. We all have an innate style. Find yours and use it to your advantage.

- Know your fear. What is your fear? Once you learn what's holding you back, you can work on it and allow your confidence to shine through. My own fear when

I was starting out in sales was asking for the order. I would be great when I met the prospect, schmoozed them, discovered their need, quoted the product, created a beautiful presentation, etc... right up until the quote was in their hands. Then I would freeze. I just didn't have the guts to say, "OK, now do I have the order?" Me, Miss Confident, glass half-full—paralyzed. But then I said to myself; what's the worst thing that's gonna happen if I ask for the order? They'll say no. So yes, my core issue was fear of rejection. Fine, I put it out there. But once I realized NO was the worst thing that was going to happen, not death, I went for it. It took me a while to drum up the confidence to come out and say, "I hope everything was to your liking. I would love the opportunity to work with you on your next event. I hope I will get the chance. Do we have a deal?"

But with practice, it came. It will come for you too.

- Sheer will and desire. There's nothing like the fire inside to get you up off the couch and pounding that pavement. If you want it badly enough, you'll make it happen. You can work hard, and work smart, but you have to want it. Truly want IT. If you don't want it badly enough, it won't work, end of story. No more discussion required.

#42: My Dad Taught Me Everything I Know About Sales, Including Integrity

Nobody makes for a better salesperson than a person with integrity. Mark my words, integrity = $$$. Call me crazy, but I'll tell you that if you keep your integrity, it will pay off handsomely. My success in business was not just due to will, fire, and passion. It was also due to my integrity. I delivered what I promised. You better believe if I made a promise to a client, I NEVER broke it. If I said I would send a catalog, I sent that catalog. If I said I would call in a week to follow up, that task would go immediately into my Blackberry. Unless someone was dying, I made that call. I ALWAYS did what I said I was going to do.

So why is integrity so crucial for sales? Having a good name is worth its weight in gold. How many times do you buy from someone because of their good reputation? You want to keep your reputation and name squeaky clean. Remember that: always have integrity in business. Even if it seems like the tougher path at times, it is the better path. Deliver what you promise, when you promise it, in the form you promised it in, for many years, and you will develop a name for yourself. This will be a major factor in contributing to your success. I promise.

#43: We Buy From People We <u>LIKE</u>: Likeability = Increased Sales

After I had scouted the marketplace high and low for all the unique ideas in my industry, at the end of the day, the majority of my products were still found at any promotional products distributor. I sold a Bic pen, and so did my competition. I could sell you 10,000 Post-it® note pads with your corporate logo, but so could Joe Schmo around the corner. So why did people REALLY buy from me? It's called the likeability factor. They sensed my passion, my love for what I was doing, and my genuine qualities as a person. They bought from me, *for* me. Unless you've created that one-in-a-million invention that's struck you that pot of gold, you're going to have competition. So be likeable. Be pleasant. Have a personality. Look like you're having fun! People don't want to do business with Mr. (or Ms.) Pessimist.

Being likable is also about being honest and genuine. If I had a bad day, I had no problem conveying that to my clients. It made me real. It made me human. People like authentic people. All these small tidbits will help you connect with your prospect along the way and make you more likeable. Try some, try all. You'll find a style that best suits you.

#44: Be Relatable (But Not Overconfident)

This is another talent that some people just possess, but it is also an acquired skill. A very good customer of mine once told me that I could chat up a homeless man on the street or the CEO of a Fortune 500 company. This is because in my life, I honestly always try to see the good in every person. There is very little that separates any of us, and life is fragile. My ability to relate to anyone has truly helped contribute to my success. Yes, I was pretty confident whenever I visited a client, but that was because I was excited to serve them. I loved what I sold, I was passionate, and I tried to be relatable. I was never cocky, obnoxious, or a "know-it-all." There's no bigger turnoff than narcissism or arrogance.

One of the reasons why I think my blog has become so widely read in the sea of women and mommy bloggers is because I'm relatable. I'm real. I'm authentic. I say it like it is. I'm fully aware of my low points and weaknesses, and I'm constantly trying to work on improving these areas. I don't have all the answers, and I think women can relate to someone who's not Miss Suzy Sunshine all the time and is still just a work in progress. So make yourself relatable. It's great to have confidence, but the line between confidence and OVERconfidence is thin. As with everything in life, try to find the balance.

#45: Fake It Till You Make It!

Have you ever been in a room where you felt like you were totally out of your league? Have you ever felt yourself surrounded by people who seem to know all the answers, and you can't come up with a single one? I can't tell you how many times, over the course of my career, I found myself in way over my head. I was surrounded by people who were way more educated, way more successful, and way more competent than me. And while I may have been having mini panic attacks at the time, I never let on that I was "less than." I always had my game face on. I mastered the art of FAKING IT!

In any business start-up, it takes TIME to master your craft and to perfect your skill. The one luxury that start-ups DON'T have on their side is that luxury of time. So if the opportunity lands on your desk, and you find yourself lucky enough to be pitching your product or service to Microsoft next week, you better be ready! You may find yourself in a position where you are just going to have to FAKE IT a little, if you don't know your stuff cold. Now there is nothing wrong with saying you don't have an answer if you don't, and you SHOULD say honestly that you don't know, if you truly don't know. My husband always used to say to me, "If you don't know, don't guess," but there is a degree of faking that will go on at the beginning of the start-up phase in order for people to buy into your product or service. Don't think for 1 minute you will not encounter this moment at one point or another in your journey. So find the inner strength, nod, smile, have your pen ready to take notes, and HIT THE INTERNET afterward to research the information you were lacking during the big moment. All these nerve-wracking moments are stepping stones and learning experiences. You'll look back on it one day and laugh.

CHAPTER 6

GROW YOUR SALES QUICKLY

As a young company, your early success can be a huge defining factor in your future success. If you have a good thing, it doesn't take long for it to spread like wildfire. If you've come up with the next cure for cancer, your sales will hit the roof in no time. But if you're like the rest of the entrepreneurs growing businesses, you will need a plan of attack. You have to create the irresistible offer. This section will provide you with lots of tips, tricks, and techniques to prepare you to grow your sales as quickly as possible. After all, what is a company without strong sales? This is probably one of the most important chapters in this guide. The next two chapters will continue with more sales and marketing strategies to grow your business quickly.

#46: Think Dr. Seuss: *Green Eggs and Ham*

You're probably wondering...what do sales have to do with *Green Eggs and Ham*? But yes, Dr. Seuss provided us with a few valuable selling tips in this book that sits on my boys' bookshelf.

For those who don't remember, here's a quick recap: basically, there are two main characters. The first character is unnamed, the second is Sam. Throughout the entire book, Sam constantly tries to get the other character to try green eggs and ham. The character refuses to taste the green eggs and ham and insists he wouldn't like them. That doesn't deter Sam from trying. Sam offers a whole list of choices, trying to persuade the character to taste the dish. After much persistence, the character finally agrees to taste Sam's green eggs and ham. A great salesman indeed!

Dr. Seuss showed us that persistence pays off in sales. Sam never gave up. He offered his prospect choice after choice, even though the prospect kept turning down those green eggs and ham. In fact, Sam offered his prospect 14 choices, until he finally closed the sale.

Now, I am not suggesting that you pester your customers and scare them away, but most unsuccessful salespeople give up way too soon in the sales process. We hear a few people say "No," and all of a sudden, we're psyched out, and we move on to the next opportunity. Yet we've merely skimmed the surface of a good (possibly a great) client. It is your responsibility as a business owner, and therefore Sales Manager as well, to ask the customer to make a decision. You cannot expect the customer to do the work for you. So think Seuss, don't let a few "Nos" psych you out. Persistence pays off.

#47: Be Exceedingly Generous About Your Salespeople's Commission Plans

If there is one lesson I've learned the hard way, it's that in life, 9 times out of 10 you get what you pay for. That being said, if you want to grow your sales, and you want your business to be more than just about you, you'll need salespeople—and good ones. In my experience, finding and keeping good people is no easy task.

So, in your search for salespeople, start-ups need to be *exceedingly generous about their commission plans*. You want hungry, dynamic, capable people, don't you? Well, you're gonna have to pay for it! Every time I tried to hire someone based solely on commission, without any base salary, draw on commission, or bonus incentive, they never worked out. I MEAN NEVER. You must pay generously for a producer, and there are usually no shortcuts. Let's go back to bullet point #20 about George Steinbrenner hiring the best for the Yankees. Now you probably don't have his budget to find and hire the best of the best right away, but his concept of paying a little extra for quality is excellent business advice. Honestly, even if your margins suffer in the short term, this is how you will grow your business. Your people are everything. You know this. Treat them with care and consider their salaries carefully.

#48: You Have to CONNECT With Your Salespeople, Even If There's Only One of Them!

I will tell you something you probably already know: happy employees are productive employees. You as the owner, as their boss, need to set the example and spread the good feelings (remember point #35). You need to connect with your salespeople, no matter how few or how many. Think back to a job you had that you loved, where you felt appreciated.

Were you good at that job? Were you productive at that job? When we like our boss and our job, we make the extra effort—for ourselves and for them. To prove this point, let's look at the flip side. Do you remember a job where you hated your boss? Did you want to give that job your all? Did you feel like trying for someone who did not appreciate your efforts? Okay, now you know the kind of boss you should be to motivate and lead your team.

Remember those Monday morning meetings over coffee and donuts I spoke about earlier? We talked as a group about how we could help each other achieve our goals. I tried to make the group feel connected, almost like a family. Family members pull their weight for each other. This is the culture in a healthy, vibrant company, and this is the culture I tried to create in my own business. When I spoke of the successes we were achieving, I spoke of OUR company's successes, not MY company's successes, and the same went for our shortcomings. My salespeople were a part of THE TEAM, in good times and in bad. As their boss, I met with each of them on a regular basis to see how I could assist them in attaining their individual goals. I made myself accessible. I knew that if I captured them, if I made them feel part of a family unit, they would be more inclined to work harder for themselves, and then for me. This all took major time, effort, and money. Plus you name it, we did it: bowling, massage therapy, drinks after work, etc. However, it paid off for me, and it will for you too. Remember, if you plant the seeds and you water and nurture this living thing called your business, it will grow and flourish.

#49: You Have to CONNECT With Your Prospect

Everything I just said applies to the client as well. You have to connect with them on that same personal level. The sooner you establish a rapport with your client on a personal level, the sooner they'll spill the beans! Like when they are going out to tender next, when they will need to restock on your merchandise, who they are currently buying from, you name it. You'll start getting some real answers. This used to come naturally to me, but it doesn't for everyone. Think about your last job; think about the suppliers you felt connected to and the suppliers you liked. Didn't you use their products or services over their competitors'? I know I did. I loved my sales rep at my pen supplier. No matter how many pen suppliers called me, I always gave Linda last refusal, and I always gave my business to Linda first. She obviously did a great job connecting with me. And these connections convert to big dollars. Don't kid yourself! You must do the same. You must connect not only with your staff, but also with the client—which leads us to the next point...who are your clients? Who do you want them to be?

#50: Make a Wish List

If you could have any client in your new business, who would it be? Have you thought about it? Have you made a list? Well, you should! In fact, you should make a "Client Wish List," and then spend your time going after those guys. I know at the beginning, we all take any order we can get our hands on just to build a portfolio. That is good and necessary. But as you progress and grow, you will need a strategy.

One of the world's largest Internet companies found me online about 8 weeks after I started my company. I was thrilled and excited when they called me to quote on the gifts for their corporate Christmas party. Talk about point #45, Fake It Till You Make It! I was talking to them like I had been in the business for 20 years. I made them feel like they could place their blind faith in me! But that's exactly what they did. When they approached me, they were certainly a wish list client of mine. I spent every reserve of energy I had to close the sale. I spent my time on that key contact, and it paid off. And then they liked my services, and referred me to another client, and on and on it rolled. But the guys who waste your time and complain and place unrealistic expectations, all for penny orders, GET RID OF 'EM! Once you have the luxury of being in business 9 months to a year, you have to start working smart. You can't simply take EVERY SINGLE ORDER. You need an action-plan when growing your sales.

#51: The Lowdown on Cold-Calling

When I conduct sales and marketing conferences, I always ask for a show of hands of who likes like cold calling. As you can imagine, very few people raise their hands. Ah, cold calling...the necessary nuisance. So if you hate cold calling, you're not alone. I actually hate being cold called myself. I can smell one a mile away. In fact, sometimes I just hang up on them right in the middle of their sentence. I always say "No, thank you," but then I hang up. I know it's rude, but obviously they haven't captivated me, otherwise we'd still be talking.

So what separates a good call from a bad one? Studies show that prospects are often willing to help the caller if it provides a means for avoiding a sales pitch. So don't get right to the pitch. Assume that this person may be only the "medium" to get you to the right person. Say something like, "I'm not sure if you're the right person to speak to about purchasing the toilet paper in your company, but if you're not, I would greatly appreciate if you could put me in touch with that person." Now, the right contact could very well be that person on the other end, but it takes them off the defensive.

Also, whenever possible, get a referral. When I first started, I literally called everyone I knew. And if my dad had friends in high places, I used it to my advantage! I would start off saying something like this: "Hi, I got your name from John Doe. I am his daughter, and he told me that you were the guy in charge of purchasing your company's promotional products. Can I just take a minute of your time?" Cold calling with a referral is a lot easier and has a much higher success rate. So when considering cold calling, the first thing I tell every entrepreneur to do is to make a list of everyone they know and start with those people. There's nothing wrong with accepting help in getting your foot in that front door. Remember, once you're in, you're still going to have to KEEP that foot in.

Another tip about cold calling is to try and pencil in a fixed time each week when you're going to do it. Otherwise, you never will. And there is no more crucial time to be proactive than right at the start-up phase, when no one knows you, and you don't yet have any built-in referrals. I recommend at least 3 times a week. I used to tell my salespeople to never do cold calls on Monday mornings, because people are catching up on e-mails, attending meetings and can have those Monday morning blues. You may catch someone at the wrong time. On Friday mornings, on the other hand, people are usually cheerful and in a good mood, so make sure to call between 9:30 and 10:30 AM that day. Shut the world out for an hour and get on the phones! You need to bring in the bacon, honey!

#52: Sales Contact Management Systems: A MUST For Growing Businesses!

If you think you are going to stay on top of EVERY sales opportunity you have now, and in the future, without the help of a system, then you're not expecting a lot of sales! When I was running my company, we were all running Symantec ACT on our PCs. There are many contact management systems on the market that allow you to stay on top of all your sales opportunities and leads. These programs allow you to set alarms for sales calls and follow-ups. You can enter pending quotes and even insert a date and follow-up time as a reminder to call a client about a particular project. It's very user-friendly and is a must-have in order to stay on top of everything and everyone. I could never have run my business without it, and my salespeople could never have stayed on top of their sales opportunities either. It was our gold. So ladies, go Google "Contact Management Software" or "Contact and Customer Relationship Management (CRM)," and find the best one suited for you. You will be amazed at its power and how productive it will make you as a company.

#53: Always Be Scouting New Products and Services

If you're selling something that everyone has, and you don't have ANYTHING unique to offer, well, that's no good, right? I used to lie awake at night consumed with trying to come up with new, unique, and different products and services to sell. Even if you only find a unique and different way to sell your existing product, that's fine too. Remember your Unique Selling Proposition (Tip #13)? A good reason to always be scouting new ideas is that when you have a new or innovative product to talk about, the spotlight is on you. And remember, everyone wants to align with a winner!

Another important advantage to finding those unique offerings is when you capitalize on something so different that no one else has, you can corner the market and set your price at whatever number you want. This is called a monopoly. It's rare, but it's golden. If you're lucky enough to have a monopoly in the marketplace, you're in the driver's seat, my friend.

#54: ABS—Always Be Selling

When you're an entrepreneur, sales don't stop after hours. An entrepreneur is more than a 9-to-5 salesperson. As entrepreneurs, we must think outside of the box. We must be creative. Now, I don't mean to be pushing product incessantly in an annoying way to people who aren't interested in what you're offering. I mean, whether you're sitting on the subway or out for dinner, never be

afraid to talk about what you're doing. I
can't tell you how many times I have
witnessed the success of this technique
first hand for myself, my husband, and
my dad. I can recall countless times I
went out for a drink, and being the
outgoing person that I am, I struck up a
conversation with the person sitting next
to me—only to find out that they were
the head of purchasing at a company on
my wish list! I used to wonder, "Is this
my lucky day or what?" Then I realized
that this actually took a lot of calculated
effort. It wasn't simply luck. It was one
part timing, one part the laws of
attraction, and one part that I was simply
always selling. The more receptive and
open I was to people, the greater my sales
grew, and the more often these types of
random meetings happened.

Remember, people buy from people they
like, so take advantage of those random
meetings and turn those friends into
customers. There's nothing wrong with
this approach. Don't look at it as a
negative. When you spread the good

feelings about what you're doing, eventually you're gonna hit the right person at the perfect time, and how sweet it will be.

CHAPTER 7

DEVELOP THE "KILLER" MARKETING PLAN

Marketing is very closely tied to sales. Because sales are so vital to the growth of a company, in this guide the sales and marketing tips spill over into three chapters (Chapters 6 through 8). Remember: to grow your sales, you will have to keep your audience (no matter who they are) interested enough to keep visiting your business or website frequently. I never liked the one-time clients. In fact, if I made one sale and didn't hear back from a client for a while, they would get the "Was something wrong with your order" call. I knew I was doing my job properly when I got REPEAT business. The key to creating the snowball effect, whereby one happy client tells another—and the synergy of it all—is in the marketing. You need a marketing plan, no matter how big or small you are, and no matter if you're selling toilet paper or opening a spa. Grab a pen...

#55: Your Website—Your Welcome Mat

First impressions are crucial in business. In fact, many of your prospects, even before meeting you for the first time, will probably Google you and your business. Therefore, your website is your welcome mat.

Depending on your business, there are lots of ways to create great-looking yet inexpensive websites. In fact, you can even go to WordPress.com or Blogger.com and create one yourself for free (you can also create more than just a blog there). My first blog was a WordPress blog. It looked professional, and I got lots of traffic. In fact, I never even took it down. It's still up! There are many different free templates and themes to choose from, and you can create something very clean and professional looking, using widgets and other great features. These platforms host your site for you, and there is no charge. In 20 minutes, you can have yourself a great-looking website.

Obviously if you are a web-based business, I would suggest hosting your own site instead of going the free route. Also, if you ever decide to monetize your site (i.e., bring in revenue through advertisements) like me, most of the free platforms do not allow advertisements.

Your choice depends on your goal, but one thing is certain; no matter how big or small your company is, you NEED a website, and it MUST look professional. No exceptions.

#56: Social Media... Hop On Board ASAP!

This is key. If you've been too afraid to dabble, now is the time. A Facebook fan page, Twitter account, MySpace account, LinkedIn profile, YouTube account, StumbleUpon account, Reddit account, Digg Account, Delicious account, ALL MUST-HAVES! Are you dizzy yet? Create them and have them linked to one another. Link them to your website. Become viral on the Internet immediately. This is vital in complementing your cold calling, referrals, and direct sales techniques. Sit at home and literally SUBMIT YOUR URL EVERYWHERE. You want Google to crawl through your site and index you. You want people to find you!

I am AMAZED every day at the power of social media. I am living proof of its vast reach, and I cannot believe the impact it has had on the success of my blog. If you don't understand its power, let me give one example. After I publish a blog post, it automatically gets uploaded to Twitter. Now, if someone stumbles upon my article, and they like it, and they reTweet it (i.e., they suggest it to their readers), I have just touched a whole new audience that I couldn't have reached on my own (possibly 100,000 new people), and it snowballs from there. Do you see the effect? Hop on the board the Social Media bus. Now is the time!

#57: Cross-promote

This is easy and very effective in getting your name out there. Have you ever offered to help a friend, and she helped you in return? Well, it works the same way in business. A great way to get your new business some attention is to choose an industry or a specific company that COMPLEMENTS your product or service, and advertise for each other. The key word is complements, not competes.

I'll give you an example of the power of cross-promotion. When I ran my business, I had a friend who owned a graphic design company. We were both targeting the same clients—him for website design, and me for promotional items. So what did we do? We helped each other grow our businesses. We put reciprocal links on each other's websites, and we had each other's business cards visible in our offices. We shared referrals, and we sent clients each other's way. Do you get where I'm going with this? It was the perfect marriage and pairing of two companies. It made us both look like a "one-stop shop," and it brought us each new opportunities that perhaps we wouldn't have reached on our own. Cross-promoting is an easy and effective way to tap into new markets.

As another example: if you own an organic food company, your business cards and flyers should be at every gym and personal training studio in the city, with a coupon to save on people's next purchase. Catch my drift?

So find a few companies or industries at the beginning that complement yours and see if you can set up a business partnership. I cannot stress enough the benefit of this setup. And go ahead and Cross-Tweet in Twitter as well! It works the exact same way in Social Media!

#58: The Power of the Internet

When I set up my Contact Management System (see point #52), I built a database of both clients and leads. Once a month, I sent out a newsletter. In that newsletter, I included a featured item of the month, recent news about the industry, and anything valuable I thought my clients would want to know. I also tried to educate my clients and give them information I thought would be useful and appropriate. I even sometimes picked a "Client of the Month" to spotlight different companies. I always had an unsubscribe button, so if they opted out, fine. Newsletters are a great way to keep your clients informed and connected. It's a value-added service that you can offer.

There are many companies who you can outsource newsletters to at an inexpensive price, if it's not your thing. I created all my own newsletters, but I paid a yearly fee to have access to different templates, as well as the hub with which to send the e-mails. But the clients appreciated it, and it put me in their face often. It was a reminder that I was always there, waiting for their business. It was a passive sell, but nevertheless, it was still a sales attempt. Consider sending newsletters once a month.

But the key in all of this marketing is the FOLLOW UP. Choose 15 of your best clients or leads to call a few days after you create your media blitz. What did they think of the featured item and price? Are they working on anything at the moment that you can assist them with? Always be around. Always follow up.

Also, online contests are great and keep the clients involved. How about a poll on your site asking your clients to make suggestions for the next item of the month, or for their input? Make it simple. Make it a multiple choice question if you like. You'd be surprised at all the useful information your clients will provide you with. You have it, so use it to your advantage! Knowledge is power.

#59: PR/Media Support: Your Way to Booming Sales, Plus It's Free!

It's free and the best kind of advertising a gal can get! Call your local papers, radio stations, and TV networks, and give them a reason to write and talk about you! Don't forget to include your website so people can check out what you're doing. I'm not floating my own boat, but I was featured in many publications and well as on television. You name it, I was everywhere. This kind of exposure did major things for my sales.

So get out there! It's a scary place to be, but it will have a direct impact on your growth. You are in business to make a buck, aren't you? You gotta do what you can with what you got. If you're not in a position to hire a whole media team, do the work yourself. Make those calls. You can be just as effective. What are you waiting for? CBS and FOX are awaiting your phone call!!

#60: Direct Marketing—The Way to Go in the Beginning

Ladies, you're a start-up. Don't play like the big boys. You'll never compete. Spending thousands of dollars on radio ad campaigns or newspaper and magazine ads to reach the masses is terribly expensive. Save that for down the road, if you should so choose. Instead, opt for some direct marketing.

What is a direct marketing campaign? Well, when you start your business, you should choose a potential target market or industry that you think will be a heavy user of your product or service. For me, it was the financial and healthcare sectors. What is it for you? When you identify this market, a direct mailing will let you test this marketplace to confirm if's actually the goldmine you think it is.

Now, when creating your ad for this specific target market, try to think outside the box. Maybe a four-color glossy postcard delivered to these prospects is a great way to get their attention and convince people to try you. Try and put a few customer testimonials on the ad, along with your key attributes. Also, your accomplishments as a company should go on every piece of literature you send out. Have you previously won a prestigious award? Have you been nominated or recognized for something? Put those in! Come up with a catchy slogan or an eye-catching design. And always give a coupon number or something you can track back to the particular campaign.

You can buy lists of businesses by industry or in your area from your local post office. Database service companies sell them as well. Create a tailored and specific ad campaign for your target market and test the waters. See what happens. Remember Chapter 3: THINK BIG, START SMALL.

#61: Don't Let the Competition Scare You

Have you ever thought of yourself as a spy? Maybe not, but there's a first for everything! You may get sick to your stomach, but you must spy on your competition. I'm not telling you to take your eye off the ball. I'm saying get acquainted with what your competition is doing. You may pick up a great tip or two and choose to incorporate it into your own business in a slightly different way.

I roamed my competitors' websites all the time. It made me dizzy, but I did it nevertheless. Often, I still thought I had a great spin on things, but I usually left their websites with one new and fresh idea I could incorporate into my own sales pitch or website. It's a great exercise, and it's never to copy, by the way. Copying is not the way to go. It's to awaken your brain and discover the possibilities. You should perform this exercise every so often, even if the thought is a little frightening.

#62: Give Freebies!

People love free stuff! You've certainly read ads that looked something like this: "The first 100 customers who visit our store get a free x." And that free thing could be ANYTHING. But the point is, people come running for freebies. I'm guilty of it, we're mostly all guilty of it. Freebies are a great way to encourage people to try out your product or service without any risk on their part.

I am also going to suggest this (not because it was my business, but because it's smart): these freebies should also include promotional products. Every time I visited a new client or prospect, I brought them a little branded item with my logo. Not a pen, or keychain, but something cool and different. Something they would use that wouldn't be just another "dust collector," and something that would remind them of me and my business, that would stay visible in their home or office. I always had tons of great promotional items lying around, branded with my logo, ready to give to leads and clients. It's all part of marketing your brand.

So remember, definitely build freebies and promotional items into your marketing budget. First, people just love freebies. Second, when you're on the golf course with a client, and they tee up their ball with your corporate logo on it, and then another potential lead finds it in the woods and then re-uses it, that's the power of the promo!

#63: Duh, Start a Blog

First, what is a blog? There are many different ways to explain what a blog is, but a blog is basically a personal journal available on the web. It's someone's personal spin on an issue, often written in casual, conversational form. Blogs are powerful because they allow you to have a voice, and your reach is boundless. A blog is a superb platform to talk about your business, your expertise, and your industry. The thing about a blog is that content is king. There is one important rule about blogging: write great content. It's really as simple as that.

Perhaps you're looking to make a name for yourself in your industry. Or perhaps you're looking for a passive income stream. There are many reasons why people start blogs. There are also a number of routes to go if you want to start to blog. Regardless, in 15 minutes anyone can set up a blog. They are free to set up, and in minutes, you're a blogger! (See tip #55 about WordPress.com or Blogger.com.) Or you can host your own site and take blogging a notch further.

Whichever path your choose, remember that people will read your blog based on its content. So become THE EXPERT in your field. Showcase your talents and opinions. Be daring or controversial.

Have the blog link back to your corporate website and vice versa. One feeds off the other, which is similar to my setup. My book feeds my blog, and my blog feeds my book. They direct people to each other. It makes me a brand. And branding is key to marketing. Blogging is also another great value-added service for your clients, who you hope will stay loyal for many years to come. Amen. That brings us to our next chapter....

CHAPTER 8

GOING THE EXTRA MILE FOR YOUR CLIENTS CONVERTS TO CASH

When you feed millions of customers around the world at thousands of locations, you know you have to keep your customers happy. McDonald's knows something about continuing to grow their sales and keeping their clients happy and loyal. Besides continuously updating their menu to satisfy society's ever-changing dietary needs, McDonald's focuses on the customer. In fact, almost any McDonald's employee can recite their mantra, the 5 Ps: People, Products, Place, Price, and Promotion. They pay careful attention to the people—both their own people, and THE PEOPLE—THE CUSTOMER. Most companies that have managed to stay afloat in our recent economic times are still in business because they have managed to meet clients' expectations. But to get ahead, you must EXCEED client expectations. A loyal client today is golden. And it's hard...you have to first find the client then stay attractive enough to keep them loyal. It's all part of increasing your sales and increasing your bottom line. ALWAYS pay attention to your clients. The client is king!

#64: Get to Know Your Customers

Understanding what makes your client tick is critical in creating customer loyalty. If you build it, he will come, but he will be more likely to come if you build it to his specifications, the way HE likes it. And I will tell you, this is not as difficult as you think. By crawling inside the minds of your clients, you will be prepared! You will be able to anticipate their moves and therefore be right there to serve them, in the best way possible.

How do you get to know your clients, so you can anticipate their needs and be there at the perfect moment to serve them when they're ready to place that order? Well, one way is by ASKING. Too often, we're afraid to ask the client what their needs are and talk too much about our own product or service. We stop listening. Learn to listen. Whenever I met a client, I always brought a pen and paper, and I always asked a few standard questions:

- What were their previous buying patterns?
- What were they displeased with in their previous buying experiences?

- And when was the next quoting opportunity?

These three questions clued me in to a lot. Their answers, combined with some chit-chat over coffee, allowed me to anticipate their moves. And there I was, happy to service them and grow my sales! So remember, get to know your customers and anticipate their moves so you can be there at the perfect moment. What's the expression? "Timing is everything," right?

#65: Exceed Expectations

Can you think back to a time where you left a particular place feeling like those people gave a darn about you? Where they bent over backwards for you? I certainly can. And you know what I did? I referred them to everyone I knew! Because for the few incredible experiences I've had with companies, or places, or restaurants, so many others have been so disappointing.

With the cut-throat competition that exists in all industries today, you simply cannot just meet expectations to stand out...you have to exceed them, as I mentioned in the introduction. After you've worked your butt off for a client, you don't want them to jump when they see the next pretty face! The first company I worked for coined a phrase: "Delight the Customer." They carefully chose that word because the word "delight" brings a smile to your face. They wanted the customer experience to be delightful from start to finish.

So once you deliver an order, ON TIME, with nothing broken, and to the client's specifications, you have met their expectations. Which is great, but there are many tricks you can perform to <u>exceed</u> their expectations. Now that you know that exceeding expectations is what you have to do in order to go the distance for your client, keep reading to learn how to wow your clients.

#66: Never Go Too Long Without Staying In Touch!

Have you ever heard the expression, "It's the little things?" Often it is the little things that make all the difference. People love to feel special. I made a habit out of never going 8 weeks without speaking to an INACTIVE client. Obviously, it was sooner than that if there was a need, but if a client of mine bought golf giveaways in April, and it was still only December, they would still get a call from me. I never stayed out of touch. I would often show up at their office out of the blue, or I would call with word that something they once bought was going on clearance. Or better, I would send them a new item with a personalized card, "Saw this and thought of you. What do you think?" You name it, I found a reason to stay in touch with my clients on a regular basis. It's all part of the job.

This shows that you care enough to make the effort. Plus it makes good, smart business sense! Timing is everything, after all, and you want your timing to be spot on, instead of too late! NEVER GO TOO LONG WITHOUT STAYING IN TOUCH. There's just too much competition today, and you're probably one of many. You have to work to keep what you got!

#67: Referral and Loyalty Programs... A Must!

I have a CIBC Visa Aerogold for one reason: I earn one air mile for every dollar I spend on this Visa. Simple. I'm loyal to the program, not to the Visa card. That's where it starts, and that's where it ends. When you're running a business, you've got to give people a reason to come back to you. There are just too many smart and savvy businesspeople out there today doing lots of crazy kosher (and not so kosher) things to keep clients. You need to create customer loyalty programs right from the start. You can be a masseuse, a distributor, a manufacturer, a cleaning service, it doesn't matter... You can create a custom-designed program for just about any business. And you must.

Because I loved the Aeroplan air miles program for the Visa card, I created that program for my own company. I let my clients earn points for every dollar they spent with us. They could collect points as they bought from us then redeem the points for gift certificates, movie passes, and other items. The grand prize after 50,000 points? A 2-night weekend stay at Mont Tremblant Resort. Sounds big, but it kept my clients loyal! If a client had to re-stock promotional items and was choosing between myself or my competitor, if they were close to reaching the next level in the point system, where do you think they would shop? That's right! For all the naysayers who dismissed loyalty programs, I thought it was a nice way to thank my clients for their loyalty.

Additionally, for each client that referred another client, they would save 10% on their next order. People love rebates and savings almost as much as freebies! You need to give people a reason to come to you, other than your great personality and gorgeous face!

#68: Some People Call It a "Bribe"... I Call It a "Thank You!"

This is going to sound tacky, but you have to make the clients your friends. It's all part of playing the game. Most of the time, I became genuinely great friends with my clients. I am still in touch with these people today, 4 years later. But I never skimped when it came to thanking them for placing their trust in me. I took them for drinks, I took them golfing, and I bought them hockey tickets. I made a 5-year anniversary cocktail at a cool bar downtown to thank them for their loyalty. Some people may call it a bribe... I prefer to call it a thank you.

I never held back when it came to my clients. Now, naturally, all these expenditures ate into my bottom line, but this was the cost/benefit to doing and keeping good business. I never took one single client for granted. They always knew how greatly they were appreciated by me and my team. Thank your clients often. They'll remember it the next time they're choosing between you and your competitor. Which brings us to our next point.. it's the little things.

#69: It's the Little Things

Some more small tricks. Besides all the contact information and quote logs you can store in your contact management software, there's also an option that lets you keep track of birthdays and anniversaries. Start from the beginning. Fill in those fields. Do the work from the start and collect all the data. Whenever it was a client's birthday, an alarm would ring from the software, and I immediately either called the client personally or sent them an e-card. They were always pleasantly surprised. These kinds of small gestures made a big impact.

My staff was encouraged to write thank you notes after an order, to make follow-up calls after an order shipped, and much more. It's not just about delivering on time and on budget, it's also about the little things.

#70: Negotiate Better Buying

We all know increasing sales is one way to drive profit. If you can grow your sales, you can most likely increase your profits. But increasing sales is not the only way to increase your bottom line. If you maintain your sales but learn how to BUY BETTER, your profits can grow even higher. How savvy are you at finding your products or raw materials at preferred prices? Pretty savvy, I hope, because it's critical to your success.

Negotiating better buying appears in this section because the lower you can buy your goods, the bigger the savings you can then pass on to your clients, which will keep them happy and loyal. It will also make you more money! In a cut-throat business, I prided myself on creating incredible supplier relationships with preferred pricing. That way, when I was competing in a bid, I had room to play with my margins. I didn't have to give my stuff away for nothing.

Being a savvy buyer is key to maintaining healthy margins and repeat business. Very important!

#71: When in Doubt, ASK!

Have you ever worked your butt off for a client, only to have them never call you again after the order was delivered? How did that feel? Did it leave you wondering what had happened and where things had gone wrong?

In many cases, clients give feedback along the way as to how we're doing. And usually, no news is good news in business! I rarely got this call from a client: "Erica, I just wanted to say thank you for a job well done." I usually only heard from the client if there was a problem. So often, we don't know what we're doing wrong or right because we have little feedback. This is why you must ask. Remember tip #64, Get to Know Your Customers?

And really, every client likes to be serviced differently. Some like to be informed along the way. Some only care that their goods or services arrive on time. So how are you going to know how to service your client? You guessed it! ASK, my friends. I briefly mentioned polls as a way to get your clients' feedback. Adding a poll to your website or blog is simple. A question like, "Which item should be featured as the 'Mother's Day Special'?" or "What's your favorite product at XYZ Co.?" Surveys are also a great way to see how you're doing in your clients' eyes. Don't be afraid to ask. I used to be afraid to ask, because I was scared of rejection. But if you don't ask, you risk not knowing. If you don't know, you risk losing clients.

#72: Wear All the Hats

When you're an entrepreneur starting a
new business, you have to wear all the
hats. Why? For most part, it's usually
because of budgetary constraints! Most
new business owners simply cannot
afford to hire the best employees right
away. They're growing and learning the
ropes themselves. So what this means is
that you will be the accountant calling for
accounts receivable one day, the sales
manager the next day, and the secretary
making coffee the next. Aren't we
women versatile?

The truth is, there's nothing wrong with
being the jack-of-all-trades at the
beginning. This lets you really learn your
business inside and out. When you've
learned Step A through Z, you're more
prepared to deal with the clients, and they
feel it. When you can get involved in
every step of an order, from accounting,
to graphics, to order processing, it keeps
you in tune with all aspects of your
business, and with the client. Knowledge

is power. I'm not saying that down the road you should be doing every position in your company yourself; that will become counterproductive. What I am saying is this: LEARN every position in your company. This was an important lesson I learned early.

CHAPTER 9

PLAN FOR THE RAINY DAY, EVEN IF IT NEVER COMES

With the debt-ridden society we live in, it seems that no one is planning for any rain (or hail) for that matter! Americans had approximately $11 trillion in national debt as of March 2009 (CBSNews.com). Trillion! Now, I assume you want your business to be a success. You're entering a boss-free zone. The sky is the limit for you, but in order to achieve all you had hoped, you must have a plan. And that plan must include a rainy day plan, even if that rainy day never comes. If you have not properly mapped out your business strategy in the greatest possible detail, you are putting yourself and your company at risk. What if your marketplace shifts and certain products become irrelevant to society? What's your plan? What if you've taken on a large office space, and your sales are not what you had forecasted? Then what? Everyone needs to plan for unexpected crises. You have to be ready.

#73: Never Assume Anything

There's an expression that goes: NEVER ASSUME, because to ASSUME is to make an ASS out of U and ME. Do you get the play on words? Often we make assumptions, and we take things for granted or accept things as true without proof. This is a grave mistake. We make assumptions such as money solves all problems, that if we work hard we're always going to succeed, or that we know what the other person is thinking. We also make strong assumptions about people in general and assume they view the world as we do. We make assumptions to make life make sense for us, to make things jive. And when we're afraid to ask questions, we just assume.

But making assumptions is very dangerous in business. You should never assume ANYTHING in business, or life for that matter. You can't assume that if you plan accordingly, everything will unfold the way you planned it. You can't assume that just because your business plan looks strong on paper, that your success is guaranteed and you'll end up on the 100 Most Powerful Women's List. Life changes on a dime, and sometimes even when we plan, our lives take a completely different path than we had anticipated.

My plans were set in stone. I "assumed" I was going to MBA School, and then after that, I would land the marketing job of my dreams. I planned everything accordingly. Well, guess what? I BOMBED my GMATS, and I didn't get into MBA School. In the end, it brought me down the path of entrepreneurship, which has been an unbelievable ride. But at the time, I was devastated. So never assume. And also don't assume that just because life doesn't work out the way you had planned, that this is a bad thing. Life always has a funny way of working out, no matter how the cards fall.

#74: DO Reinvest Profits in Your Business

So, you're showing profits in your new business. Congrats! This is wonderful. What are you going to do with this new-found money? Buy a new car, a new house, a yacht? Actually, the wisest thing you can do is reinvest those profits right back into your new business.

We've all heard the expression, "Save for a rainy day." This is how I was brought up. This is the motto my family lived by.

We always lived beneath our means, and amidst my dad's success, he always saved for a rainy day. This message stuck with me when I was running my company.

While I was neither cheap nor stingy when it came to getting the best I could afford (e.g., people, showroom, website, catalogs), I was very careful about how I spent the company's money. After I had hardly taken a salary for the first few years, the profits I made went right back into the company. The more money that stays in the business, the more your company is worth.

So because you never know what tomorrow will bring for your new business, or any business for that matter, never forget to reinvest profits. Most companies fizzle after 5 years because of the lack of necessary funds to grow. Create a Corporate Rainy Day Fund, or Slush Fund, as it's often called. If you are not a disciplined person, set up a SEPARATE account for profits, so you can't be tempted to take out those profits for your own personal good time. Nothing in life is guaranteed, and you always need to be prepared in business. Which leads us to the flip side of the coin...

#75: DON'T Reinvest All Profits in Your Business

You should be reinvesting most of your profits, especially in the early years, and you should be creating that Corporate Rainy Day Fund. However, I do believe in keeping some for yourself. Here's the BUT. If you've been able to draw a salary and are living off that salary, I do believe in taking some of the profits and INVESTING them. Girls, you need not only save for your corporate rainy day. You need to save for your PERSONAL RAINY DAY.

After a few years, when profits were increasing, I took some money out and put it toward my 401K/RRSP. I also gave some of that money to my investment adviser to invest. You could do the same. But put that money away, and FORGET YOU HAVE IT. Let it grow. Let it work for you.

Don't be tempted to take money out of your business and spend it on foolishness. If there is money left over after you have reinvested most of the profits in your business, then take some for you, but for your FUTURE. Plan. Save. This is critical. I assume you don't want to work until you're 90. You shouldn't live your life without a savings plan. Which brings us to our next planning point.

#76: Plan Ahead

Preparing for the rainy day is not just about saving and reinvesting profits. There are other kinds of rainy days. There are late deliveries that threaten the loss of a good client. There are employees that quit during critical moments. We also have certain life responsibilities as women that don't fall upon the shoulders of men. Perhaps you have an ailing mother or sister, or perhaps you have children. As businesswomen, we all need support. This is why planning ahead is so crucial.

Planning ahead applies to just about everything. If there is some good advice I can give you, it's to always plan whenever possible. Always anticipate the possibility of the unforeseen. If you have a big presentation for a key client, make sure you have a friend on call or a grandmother as backup ready to pitch in, in case you get the call that your kid barfed all over the classroom! Don't laugh. This has happened to me. Whenever I have something very big planned for the day, I always arrange coverage for my children, a friend or someone who can help out just in case. It all goes with the territory.

Another way I always prepared myself in business was I made sure I really got to know my suppliers. Get to know your suppliers well—their strengths and their weaknesses. If there is one who you like to work with but has a tendency for later deliveries, GIVE THEM AN EARLIER DEADLINE. This is a no-brainer, friends! I ALWAYS delivered on time. Why? Well, for one, it went with the whole integrity thing. (Remember tip #42?) But I was never late because I was good at organizing things behind the scenes. You need to be organized. Always tell your suppliers you need goods before you actually do. Allow room and time for error so you don't have to operate under panicked and stressful conditions. Business is stressful enough, so always plan ahead.

#77: Rainy Days Are Great Wake-Up Calls for Change

So, you're gonna plan ahead, and think that everything is gonna go smoothly. Right? Not so fast, ladies. It still won't. You're not going to be able to catch every falling star. So when the rainy day comes, look for the message. Rainy days are great wake-up calls for change.

Our Office Manager's responsibilities included accounts receivable, accounts payable, general office administration, and order follow-ups. Once the salespeople booked their orders, I wanted them booking MORE orders, so our amazing Office Manager would handle each step of their order, right up until shipment. She was doing a great job at getting the orders out on time, but I noticed in a few incidences that the logos on our items were not exactly to the clients' specifications. When this began to happen more frequently, obviously we had to find a solution, and that meant revisiting our processes. Although the salespeople were not happy when I told them that they now had to start taking care of their own artwork on every order (because they were the ones who knew the project best), they understood my reasoning. After losing a few clients due to our flawed internal order processes, these hiccups became a good wake-up call for change.

#78: Spend Less Than You Earn!

Hello, the no-brainer most people know, but don't follow! Don't get caught up keeping up with the Joneses, personally or professionally. This is a basic principle of life and money. It sounds simple, yet many people are buried in debt or spending next week's paycheck. Once you can pay off your debts and start to save again, you truly move into the driver's seat, and the world can once more become your oyster.

Besides being burdened by the weight of the debt itself, the weight of the stress is even greater. If your salary is not able to support your lifestyle, think about where you can cut...both in your personal life and in your business. There are lots of things we THINK we need that we in fact do not. So, one warning: live below your means...your business means and your personal means. Just as you make your corporate budget, you also need a personal spending budget. You should know exactly how much it costs you (and your family) to live so you know that magic figure and can avoid sinking into debt.

79: Know That Nothing Lasts Forever, Good or Bad

I sort of feel like my mom coined this phrase, though in fact she didn't. I've been hearing this statement ever since I was old enough to understand what it meant. I'll give you an example to illustrate the point. If you're the mom of a newborn, and you think you can't go one more sleepless night, BOOM, your baby starts sleeping nights! On the flip side, just when you think you have your baby going through the night, BOOM, she's waking up again! It's just the way life goes.

So if that rainy day does come, please remember these words: nothing lasts forever, good or bad. If your business slides into a funk, and so do you, know that it's not going to last forever. I'll never forget the nervous feeling I had from January to March, every year. Companies had just spent their holiday budgets, and no one was spending in the first quarter on corporate gifts. I would look at my bottom line, and I would literally panic. But come the middle of March, like clockwork, with golf season just around the corner, the phones would ring again and we'd gear up for our corporate promotional blitz. The one thing I did do during the funks was work HARDER. I literally got SCARED into the hard work. When things are rolling, we tend to ease up on the cold calls and start to become REACTIVE. Nothing like a good ol' rainy day to get you scared and PROACTIVE again. You see where I'm coming from?

#80: The F Word—Failure

Don't hate me, but I had to write a section that addressed the unwanted, the unforeseen, and the unplanned (even though I touched on it already in Tip #36). Failure—a term that takes on many different meanings and contexts. One definition of failure, and the one you are probably thinking of in reference to this book is, "The act or fact of becoming bankrupt or insolvent" (Dictionary.com). Yes, there is a chance that you will fail in your new business and not make it. It's a possibility. Anything in life can happen. But it's important not to let it dictate your life. You can't let the odds of something bad happening keep you down. That's no way to live. And chances are, if you're an entrepreneur, you won't visit that dark place too often.

If you've done the proper budgetary planning, have set up a strong marketing and sales plan of attack, assembled a good team of key players, and have a little stroke of luck on your side, you shouldn't have to think about the F word. By buying this guide, you are already committing to the cause that you want your business to succeed, and not to fail. Now, that's a step in the right direction.

#81: Always Have a Plan B... Or Not

Call it what you want—contingency plan, safety net, Plan B, whatever.

Have you ever had to turn to Plan B in your life? I didn't have a Plan B—I only had a Plan A. I remember all too clearly my life plan when I was in Psychology at McGill University for 3 years. Land a great job for 2 years for my CV. Then back to MBA School for 2 years. Then land the Big Marketing Job at a Fortune 500 Company. It sounded great on paper. My marks were strong, my first job out of school was a good one. I worked on applications for MBA School, but then, as I told you, the GMAT disaster struck. I had to look to Plan B, but the problem was, I had no Plan B. I just had a Plan A. I never had prepared myself for the rejection. So when I didn't have a Plan B, I was completely devastated and down for a long time.

Although I never had a Plan B for myself, God had a Plan B for me. And this is where I tell you to have faith that the universe will support you. It's great to plan ahead, and it's necessary to do so. It's great to anticipate what you will do if you need that backup plan. But sometimes, when we plan, God laughs. And sometimes when he laughs, things have a mysterious way of working out. My job at the Fortune 500 Company never came, but I'll tell you, once my business started really grooving, those offers poured in. And funny, I didn't want ANY of them. God's Plan B for me was far better than my own Plan A. So while we can plan and forecast most of our business decisions, some things we just can't plan. And that will have to be okay.

CHAPTER 10

THE EMOTIONAL SIDE OF BUSINESS... WE ARE WOMEN AFTER ALL!

We are women, hear us roar! Curvy, sensual, smart, passionate, capable women. Sometimes irrational, sometimes excitable. This doesn't make us flawed; it makes us women, and we wouldn't have it any other way, thank you very much! Those who think there is no room for emotion in business are quite mistaken. In fact, people are recognizing more and more the importance of emotional intelligence in the business world today. I say, don't hide behind your emotions or use them as a crutch. Make them work for you! Strut your stuff, women!

#82: Women Are Emotional Beings—This Doesn't Mean We Can't Be Successful!

A woman can do anything a man can do. There's just one tiny thing that happens to women that doesn't happen to men. We menstruate once a month! This gift that comes to us every 30 days can throw our business edge a little off-kilter...in addition to other female hormones like estrogen! Hello, we are women, after all! But this monthly friend and all the enraged hormones that accompany it should not stand in the way of your success.

Women have made incredible strides and extraordinary contributions to society,

especially in recent years. Angela
Merkel, #1 on the 100 Most Powerful
Women's list in 2009, is the Chancellor
of Germany (Forbes). Other women in
the top 25 on that list are the chief
executives of companies such as
PepsiCo, Kraft, DuPont, Sunoco, Yahoo,
Xerox, and Avon. Wow! Women are
running Corporate America! No more
information required. We hold some of
the highest-ranking positions in society
today, and our success has been growing
each year. All of these accomplishments
prove that our value has been recognized
as significant. As an advocate for women,
evidence of this success couldn't make
me any happier.

#83: Emotional Intelligence

So what is emotional intelligence, and
how does it relate to your business?
Emotional intelligence deals with the
"feeling" side of business. And it's not
only about being tuned into your own
emotions...it's about being tuned into
those around you as well. Good business

is about good communication. Management style and interpersonal skills are crucial factors in the proper running of a company. By understanding what triggers us in our business (e.g., about certain employees or clients), we are able to forecast other people's behaviors and therefore prevent our feelings from getting the best of us. By better understanding ourselves and our reactions to those around us, we can choose how we behave. This is therefore a powerful concept.

As the song goes, "The times they are a'changin." Managers used to be encouraged to hire employees based on intelligence and expertise in their fields, yet today's experts are saying that when hiring employees, you shouldn't look to only hire the smartest people. Rather, you should hire employees who show good emotional intelligence, good self-awareness, self-management, and the ability to maintain good relationships. It's very disruptive to your company to hire an employee who has little emotional intelligence. Be choosy in how you select your employees. Whether they are emotionally intelligent or not can make all the difference.

#84: Letting Emotions Get in the Way of Good Decision Making

I think as women, we often let emotions get in the way of good decision making, for whatever reason. I have been guilty of holding onto employees for way too long because I liked them as people. We are all guilty of such behavior at one point or another in our lives. But every decision you make that pertains to your business should come down to one question, and one question only: **Will this decision be good for my business?** That's where it starts, and that's where it ends. It's okay to care about other people's emotions, but it cannot weigh down your judgment for clear decision making. Robert De Niro said it best in his movie, *Heat*: "Don't allow yourself to get attached to anything you cannot walk away from in 30 seconds flat if you feel the

heat around the corner." Well said,
Mr. D.

#85: Being an Entrepreneur Will Take You Out of Your Comfort Zone

I remember my Oprah "A-HA moment,"
when after trudging along to write the
business plan, get funding, create a
website, etc., I woke up in a sweat at 3:15
AM; I realized the seriousness of what I
was doing. If things didn't work out, I
was liable for $100,000. (Remember tip
#23?) That's pretty intense for an
unmarried 24-year-old woman. To be
frank, I was scared shitless.

Becoming an entrepreneur and feeling
like you have the weight of the world on
your shoulders can be emotionally nerve-
wracking. You'll probably have rent,
suppliers to pay, employees' salaries, and
more. It's a lot. But then again, if you
never risk, and you live forever in your
comfort zone, chances are you'll never
know true success. Part of becoming an
entrepreneur is being taken out of that

comfort zone and becoming comfortable with the uncomfortable. It takes time and practice, but it's all part of the job! The job you signed up for, remember? ☺

#86: The Disease to Please

I am a pleaser. Maybe it's a female thing, maybe it's a me thing. When people visit my home, I like to make sure they're comfortable. I try to be likeable. I try to be a good and loyal friend. I aim to please! I did the same with my customers and employees. I always tried to accommodate them and make them happy. The problem was that I was becoming a human pretzel! Sometimes pleasing goes overboard and starts to become a disease. Yes, the disease to please.

And while I'm still somewhat of a pleaser, I've gotten better at doing what's best for the cause. Girls, remember, at the end of the day in your business, it's about dollar signs. I made my employees my friends because of this disease to please and ended up keeping underperforming employees on for way too long. This in turn negatively affected productivity, and therefore the bottom line. It did not serve me well at all. Shake your disease to please, and quickly.

#87: The Buddy System

I believe in never suffering alone. I believe all women need support in order to thrive. I have a loving family and a lot of girlfriends who have offered me support in dark times. Why should it not apply in business? You may find yourself in a position where you just can't unlock the answer and could use a friend's listening ear. Sometimes the best medicine is a buddy—another female in the same boat as you, to help you through your situation as an objective person.

Pick a buddy. She can be your best friend or she can be someone you know from a baby group class. She could be someone you met at a networking cocktail party. Your buddy should be someone you respect and can count on for support. She can be in the same field of work as you, or not. Sharing your goals, successes, and issues is a great way to release some stress and make sure you're heading in the right direction.

It has been written that Bill Gates and Warren Buffet are business buddies and bounce ideas off one another. I have no confirmation whether this is the truth, but imagine being a fly on the wall in that boardroom. Talk about creative juices flowing!

Running a business is no small feat. Get a buddy. And if you like how that's going, expand on the duo to create a group.

#88: Starting Your Business Takes Emotional Energy and Commitment

Besides hard work, timing, and a stroke of luck, starting your business also takes commitment—in every sense of the word. One characteristic of all successful entrepreneurs is the unconditional commitment to succeeding, no matter the cost. Martha Stewart and Oprah Winfrey are dedicated to their cause. They are virtually married to their careers, which take up a tremendous amount of time, energy, and commitment. But it is a key ingredient in becoming successful.

Businesses have ups and downs. The emotional side to this is you must be ready to ride the roller coaster and stay steady all the while. You must be committed. I can recall so many times when I broke down crying in my office out of sheer frustration. I closed my door, and the floodgates opened. Either a client was unhappy with an order, or an employee did something that upset me, and it emotionally drained me. But at the end of the day, you are the leader, and you must rule with your head. There is room for the heart (and you must have heart), but it's nothing personal. It's just business.

#89: How to Deal with Feeling Overwhelmed (Because It Will Happen)

All of us have felt overwhelmed at certain times in our lives. It's called life, and sometimes our emotions can go into overdrive. We've all felt frustrated or overwhelmed about our jobs, our kids, or just life in general. Feeling overwhelmed can cloud your judgment and prevent good decision-making. You must nip feeling overwhelmed in the bud the minute it creeps into your life. Let me offer a few tips that will help prevent the drive into Overwhelm Central:

- Practice good time management. Make to-do lists and schedule realistic tasks for yourself on any given day. And amidst all the work, give yourself enough time to eat a good, healthy lunch each day. Proper nutrition is of great importance. It's your fuel for regrouping; it gives you a chance to walk away, re-balance, and come back refreshed. I never skipped ONE lunch. You are a person, not a machine.

- Prioritize. Not all things are created equal. This means you must prioritize and conquer your tasks according to importance. Get the biggest tasks out of the way, and get the ones with the soonest deadlines out of the way. Organizing your filing cabinet is pressing, but definitely not as pressing as getting out an order that is due in 48 hours.

- Take a break. Physical and mental. It goes beyond never skipping lunch. I often went for short, brisk walks on my lunch hour. I kept my running shoes at my desk or in my car. I sometimes closed my eyes and meditated. You're the boss; you can close your door at whatever moment you choose. Close your door, close your eyes, and practice eight slow breaths in for a count of eight, and out for a count of eight. And realize, NOTHING IS LIFE OR DEATH. This puts things into perspective and reduces those feelings of being overwhelmed.

#90: Make a Worry List

When I was in year 3 of my business, and things started to really pick up, I began to burn out. I ended up in therapy, and I needed help badly. My brain was not shutting off at night, and I would lie awake in bed, mind racing, exhausted, unable to stop obsessing about work. I wasn't becoming emotional ABOUT work. I was becoming emotional FROM work.

My therapist gave me the best advice I can give anyone who has started to let their business consume them. Start a WORRY LIST. This is simply a pen and paper that you leave on your night table or in your purse. Any time you feel yourself becoming overwhelmed about things that worry you, take it off your brain and put it on a piece of paper. I would allow myself a few times in the day to have my "worry period" and then it was over. I would then carry on with my day. But that worry list and worry period literally saved me from my sleepless nights. I got it out of my head and onto paper to deal with at a better time, when I was in a better frame of mind to go through my issues. Be careful of burnout, ladies. Entrepreneurs have a tendency to GO GO GO. Burnout can creep up out of nowhere. Sometimes we need to slow down, regroup, and take a break. Which brings us to our final chapter... how to balance it all!

CHAPTER 11

BALANCING IT ALL... LIFE, LOVE, FAMILY, KIDS, AND THE BUSINESS

This is by far both my favorite section and my biggest challenge: the endless juggle. The daily grind. The attempt at being superwoman. At the end of the day, life is about making everything work. So, if you are going to be uni-dimensional and let this business consume you,

you've ignored the message. Life is a journey, and I want you to enjoy every step along the way. You should celebrate the milestones with your partner, and you should take a day off to regroup with your friends or family. You must learn the art of the juggle and how to make the business fit in with your life. Because what's a life without balance and congruence? You may not be able to have it all at the same time, but that doesn't mean you shouldn't strive for balance.

So, congratulations, you've made it to the last chapter! You read through the business nitty gritty sections. This is your life section, where you make it all come together and work for you. Grab a coffee and enjoy this chapter. It's for you to truly reflect and set your priorities.

#91: Put Yourself Back On Your To-Do List

The start-up phase is both difficult and intense. It's physically and emotionally exhausting and takes much out of you.

All the running, all the planning, making sure you have the proper systems and people in place to be successful. You also have demands at home. Perhaps you have a significant other, kids, parents to care for, or all of the above. All of these intense demands placed upon ourselves have put us last on our to-do lists. This is a grave mistake. It's normal for it to happen, but I urge you to put yourself back on your priority list. After all, if you don't care for yourself, you will have a hard time caring for those around you.

You MUST find the time to do the things you love. Revisit them and don't forget about them. It's going to feel all-consuming at the beginning until you find your groove. But go for walks, take that hot bath, treat yourself to a manicure, take a stroll with a coffee and visit the bookstore, go for a girl's night out, go to the gym, go to bed early. Whatever self-care means to you. It is crucial you do not give up the things that bring balance to your life and help you juggle this new beast called entrepreneurship that has invaded your life.

#92: Set Your Priorities—Family Comes First

Family comes first on the priority chain. It must. Please do not ever lose sight of this. It's very easy to let the business take over your life and fully consume you. When you're finally home, stay emotionally present. Don't let the work invade your personal space. Your family needs you. Your partner needs you. Your children desperately need you.

I had a guest blogger on my site discuss this mobile madness that is so dangerously invading our family lives. It's the concept that our Blackberries, iPhones and computers are always on, always around, and there are no etiquette rules in how to use this new technology. As a result, people are on their Blackberries texting and e-mailing constantly during precious moments with their kids. We've all been guilty of it at one time or another, I know. But ladies, our families have eyes, and they have feelings. When you're home, stay emotionally home. I know you want your businesses to thrive, but FAMILY COMES FIRST.

#93: The Hubby or "Significant Other" Section

Okay, you can skip this section if you're not married or in a committed relationship. Yes, your man has a whole section all to himself. I made this his section because besides having to be there for our children, our partners need us more than we realize. Without keeping your relationship intact, you'll end up enjoying your successful business...ALL ALONE.

I made this mistake along the way. I became too consumed with my business. I stayed awake at night, and instead of bonding with my wonderful husband, I was on the computer, submitting my URL, researching new and unique products, and checking out my competition. I isolated myself, and he started to feel lonely. I felt it. I knew it was wrong, but I kept saying to him, "I want so badly to make this business a go. I desperately need it to be successful," until I saw that it was not taking us down a good path.

So remember your priorities. The rules apply to your partner as well. I'll say it again: when you're home, stay home with your man. You have to keep the passion alive. He is your partner, after all, and he has to be your best friend. Why not include him in your journey and bounce some ideas off of him? You never know...he may become just as passionate about your business as you are. He wants your success. Let him in. Love your partner. There is room for everything. You just have to MAKE the room.

#94: Is There Really Such a Thing as "Having It All"?

So, is there such a thing? Can women have it all? Of course women CAN'T have it all! You tell me one person who has absolutely everything! Perfectionism is an illusion of the mind. I wrote a blog post about the women who try and have it all, and then go into therapy when they realize that it's virtually impossible.

Over the past few decades, women's contributions to society have been remarkable. We make up half the US workforce, and are holding some of the highest-level positions in the country (as I mentioned in Tip #82). However, if I show you studies of 300 highly paid female executives who seem to have it all, marriage, kids, great career, money, 87% of them are considering making a life-altering change. **Eighty-seven percent!** (New York's Yankelovich Partners). Studies also show that these women crave more balance, less pressure, a lighter workload and more time at time, and are leaving corporate America in large numbers to either stay home or start their own businesses.

So, let's first take a look at what it means to **have it all**. For me, Oprah represented having it all. A dream job, power, success, and friends in high places. But then I got married, and I had babies who threw up on me, peed on me, and caused me sleep deprivation. I soon realized that Oprah is missing a major component in life. She never married or had kids amidst all her success. She also probably has very little "me" time or privacy. Maybe she even feels lonely or isolated at the top. So truly, who has absolutely everything?

Having it all means being happy and balanced, truly content from within, regardless of how much money you have, regardless of whether you work, stay home, or opt out of motherhood altogether. Hey, we all have something to deal with. If life doesn't get you one way, it gets you another. You could have all the money and power in the world and have a sick child, for example. Or you can have a rich life surrounded by incredible family and friends and joy, but struggle monetarily. So learn to love what you have.

And remember, perfection is an illusion. I think it's okay that most women can't have it all. It doesn't make us flawed. It just makes us human.

#95: Learn the Art of Saying the Forbidden Word, "NO"

As working women, as single moms, as wives, as friends, we're pulled every day in a thousand different directions. I'm not saying we don't have responsibilities we are unable to escape in our daily lives. What I am saying, is if you feel like your plate is already full, now is not the time to pile more on it. And saying no takes practice. Saying no to friends, no to husbands, no to clients, no to employees, no to charities, no to someone asking you for a loan, no to a bothersome person, no to an incredible opportunity…because now just may not be the ideal time for you.

If you feel like you're becoming a human pretzel, just a few words of advice. But first, before I do, I would like to clarify that I am not saying you should be selfish and never help people out. However, starting a business is a **major** undertaking, and you will not be able to say yes to everyone and everything. So get it out of your head that you can do everything and be everywhere. Something's gotta give.

- Think back to a time when you were turned down or rejected yourself. Did you die from it? Of course you survived it! Don't assume you're going to inflict serious harm by saying no to someone. Saying no is a part of everyday life. Take it all in stride. If you do, you'll be easily able to say no to others, which means YES to yourself.

- Saying no without any guilt is quite uncommon, but say it when you need to say it. To your children, to your spouse, to your boyfriend, to your employee. What's your human pretzel threshold? Are you there yet?

- Don't instinctively say yes. Think it out first. It's okay not to answer on the spot. How about something like, "Can I think it over and get back to you?" If anything, you sound more mature, professional, and if it really ends up being a no, it will sound like a better, more thought-out no. And may I also note, you don't have to be rude when you say no either. You should say it politely, thank you very much!

- And finally, if you do say yes, and then you feel resentment, it means you SHOULD HAVE SAID NO!

So, say NO, and let it be guilt free...except for sex with your partner...I say go for it!

#96: Girlfriends—We Need Them as Our Sounding Boards

If there is one group of people besides my incredible family that has nourished my soul more during stressful times, it's my girlfriends. Don't ignore them! While our husbands or partners can be there for us in a way that many cannot, our girlfriends fill a void that our partners cannot. They are not mutually exclusive, and you shouldn't have to live without either one.

There's nothing like having a crappy day at the office, and then a drink with the ladies at the end of that day to make the "boo boos" go away. The laughter is intoxicating and so healthy for your body. Your girlfriends will put perspective on your life that you didn't see possible. So, while we have friends

for a reason or a season, never lose touch
with your friends. Make the time.

#97: You Gotta Move

Ladies, you're starting a business. You're
becoming an entrepreneur. You've got a
lot on your plate! I have worked with
many female entrepreneurs. The
beginning is rough. There are days where
the hours are so long, from reading over
your business plan, to interviewing staff
and budgeting, that the gym becomes the
LAST thing on your mind. Maybe you
just want to "kerplunk" on the floor at the
end of your day. All the running from
work, to meetings, chasing your kids,
trying to find the time and energy to
reconnect with your husbands...the daily
grind definitely takes its toll.

If you're like me, then getting to the gym
can be a real chore. Especially now that
I'm blogging (and writing this book), I
have come up with nearly every excuse in
the book to avoid the gym. "I haven't
written a blog in a couple of days, so I

want to write one this morning. I have no time for the gym today!" But I make the time. I make it a priority. It's all part of the balance, and it's there for my mental and physical well- being.

A few things you NEED to do for yourself.

1. **Try to exercise 3 to 5 times a week.** Make it a priority and write it or enter it in your planner, Blackberry or calendar. That should be your goal. This means that at the gym, outside, in your basement, or at the office, you are choosing to be physically active for an hour 3 to 5 times per week. It doesn't matter where. And it doesn't matter when. I prefer to work out in the morning, but many people love lunch-hour workouts, and most like it after work. A mix of cardio and strength training is best. You will feel simply divine afterward. I promise.

2. **Don't be lazy.** There are benefits to doing tasks in an "unlazy" manner; taking the stairs instead of the elevator, walking at lunchtime, walking to the pharmacy or post office, biking to the office. Seriously, you have to get to these places anyway, so you may as well burn some extra calories in the process.

3. **A few notes on calories burned.**
Biking–leisurely pace for 1 hour 230–340 calories burned
Walking–Moderate pace 1 hour 205–300 calories burned
Mowing the lawn per 1 hour 300–450 calories burned
Jogging–Moderate pace 1 hour 300–600 calories burned

4. **Invest in a yoga mat.** Keep it in your car or somewhere handy. Check out some of the local yoga studios and their class schedules. Try Pilates or Zumba (a type of Latino dancing). You will notice both a physical and mental difference in your mind and body.

Don't be quick to say no. When I start my day out with yoga, I am balanced, calm, and energized.

5. **Sleep. Get 8 to 10 hours a night of shut-eye time if you can.** Sleep has much to do with staying mentally and physically fit. If you sleep, you will have greater energy to exercise and work, and this surge of energy will follow you in all areas of your life. If you're not getting enough, try programming your body by closing your eyes 10 minutes earlier each night until a pattern develops.

6. **Cut out booze and cigarettes.** We often hear that alcohol is "Fattening." It's not called the "Silent Assassin" for nothing. But besides cutting out booze for calories, you will feel less sluggish the next day. Same goes for cigarettes. Quit, quit, QUIT!

Moving your body in any way releases endorphins (the good hormones) and decreases serotonin levels (the bad hormones). Make the time to move.

#98: The Art of Surrender

I owe my mother a huge thanks for this section. Whoever said balancing it all is easy? When you are a Type-A personality like me, and an overachiever, it can be frustrating when you realize you are not Superwoman. So, my aim in this section is to help you engage in the **act of surrendering**, to truly surrender yourself to the control of life.

For years, I never surrendered. I pushed as hard as I could. I went as quickly as I could. And I was pretty good at it too. I got so frustrated with slow responses, slow people. In fact, when I was running the business, most of my days were spent frustrated, waiting for an answer from a supplier or waiting for people I thought were incompetent. As I've said, I was burning a lot of negative energy. I ended up in therapy because of it. I stopped sleeping. I was all-consumed with work and doing the best job I could, until my therapist told me that my behavior was not serving me well, in the least bit. And if I kept it up, I was heading into a full-blown burn-out.

So, after months of therapy (and much money spent), my mom, my second therapist, took over! She taught me the art of surrendering: surrendering to life. Life really is a juggling act. A balancing act. It's not about finishing first, or finishing best. It's about being steady. I felt so caught up in the expectations I had placed on myself that I felt constantly disappointed. Once I learned to surrender to the illusion of perfection and accepted that I wasn't going to be my best every day, and that some things would have to wait, I started to relax a little. I started to get healthier in my head and in my heart. I felt free. I truly did.

Once I got the hang of it, I REALLY started to surrender. And it felt YAHOO great! Hey, my kids are only young once. That e-mail would have to wait until tomorrow once I got home from the office. My house would get a little messy on the weekend, and thankfully, no one would die because of it. My presentation for the client wasn't my best ever, but hey, that stuff happens! All with a grain of salt, ladies.

#99: Work Hard, Play Hard, and Have Fun!

Congrats. You breezed through 99 points! I hope you learned some tips and tricks that are going to take you through one of your greatest life adventures. Remember, we only get one chance on this earth, so make it count. Make it great. Life is no dress rehearsal, and because you're an entrepreneur, you already know this. You're going to work your butt off, but it's going to feel rewarding. There are no shortcuts. So enjoy your journey. Have fun. Enjoy each high and each low. Go steady. Go slowly. Go with care. I'll be there with you in spirit, your cheering squad, waiting for you at the finish line.

APPENDIX:

WORKSHEETS

Checklists

Unlocking your passion:

What is your passion?

What are your hobbies?

What are you good at?

Building your Business Plan:

Have you gone to your local bank and picked up a business plan information pamphlet?

Business plan checklist:

- ✓ Executive Summary: **Some highlights of your business**

- ✓ **Company Description**: Describe your business and plans for your start-up

- ✓ **Product or Service**: What are you selling? Focus on the benefits.

- ✓ **Market Strategies:** Define your target market.

- ✓ **Competitive Analysis:** What makes your idea different and competitive?

✓ **Strategy and Implementation**: You must be specific. How are you going to take your business from conception to a full-fledged, running business?

✓ **Web Plan Summary**: Sales and marketing strategies and how you will go to market online. You can't ignore the power of the Web today.

✓ **Operations and Management plan**: Discuss the management and business day-to-day functioning plan.

✓ **Financial Analysis**: Profit and Loss, Cash Flow predictions. All financials.

In one sentence, what's your competitive edge?

Have you thought of a charity you want to tie your business to? Don't forget that you have to give back!

Have you started looking for a mentor? Take to your community, surf the Web! Find yourself a mentor.

Did you practice the art of positive thinking today?

Have you made your vision board yet?

Have you made it a point to attend at least 1 to 2 networking events this week?

Have you found the best salespeople that you can afford?

Have you given them any incentive to chase the business?

Do they receive any bonuses if they sell more? Don't forget to tease them with a little reward for surpassing goals.

Did you make your wish list of clients you are going to target in the immediate future?

Your cold call list: Did you set aside at least 3 hours this week for cold calling? Get on those phones!

Did you leave yourself time this week to look for more innovative products or services to sell?

Is your website up to par with those of other companies in your industry? Word of mouth is a great way to find yourself a web designer to create your site.

Have you created a Facebook fan page, Twitter account, MySpace account, LinkedIn profile, YouTube account, StumbleUpon account, Reddit account, Digg Account, Delicious account?

Have you hooked up with a company to CROSS-PROMOTE with?

Have you called your local newspaper and radio stations and even TV stations and given them a reason to cover you in the media?

Have you recently spied on your competition?

Have you started a Blog? Visit WordPress.com or Blogger.com today!

Have you called up your clients recently and asked them how you're doing and if you're satisfying their needs? Ask for feedback!

Have you created some sort of customer loyalty program to reward clients for using your product or service?

Have you done any of "The Little Things" lately to thank the clients you currently have?

Have you called your suppliers back and confirmed you are getting your goods and services at the best possible price? Renegotiate pricing.

Have you learned all aspects of your business, even if those responsibilities will not be yours going forward?

Have you created your corporate rainy day plan?

Do you have a Plan B in the event that your business does not make it?

When making a recent decision, did you make the decision by answering the following question: WILL THIS DECISION BE GOOD FOR MY BUSINESS? When in doubt, this is the question you need to be answering.

Did you find yourself a business buddy?

Have you put yourself back on your to-do list? Made time for the gym, for a walk, for a coffee with a girlfriend? If not, you must!

Have you been saying yes when you wanted to say no? Say NO the next time you want to, and say it without any guilt.

Have you gone to the gym or for a walk outside lately? It will clear your thinking. You've gotta move!

Notes to self:

Notes to self:

Notes to self:

Notes to self:

Notes to self:

Notes to self:

ABOUT

THE

AUTHOR

ERICA DIAMOND

With almost 20 years of sales experience and 15 years of marketing experience, Erica Diamond is a born entrepreneur. Using a small savings from her first job as a marketing manager at a large corporation, Erica built her promotional products Company, Unique Corporate Gifts, from scratch at 24 years old.

After enjoying 7 years of great financial success with her company, Erica sold her business in 2006 to Canada's largest bag retail chain. Her business journey along the way has resulted in a ProMontreal Young Entrepreneur Award, a Top 30 under 30 Entrepreneur Award, a Top 40 under 40 Entrepreneur Award nomination, among numerous others, and finally, The Profit Hot 50 Award for owning One of Canada's 50 Emerging Growth Companies. She was the only female CEO on this list. Erica has also been featured on the cover of the business section of multiple newspapers, other publications and has made TV appearances.

Fast forward to September 2009 and the birth of Women On The Fence (www.WomenOnTheFence.com). This is the blog that Erica had only dreamed of creating and is now finally a reality. Women come from all around the world by the thousands to feel connected and inspired, to better understand their own life experiences, to laugh and to cry.

In the short time that she has run the blog, Erica has been featured on Blogher.com, Wordpress.com, Woman.ca, and TwitterMoms.com. She blogs for celebrity mom Brooke Burke's ModernMom.com. Her blog was recently monetized by one of the world's largest Media Companies, Glam Media. Erica was also recently appointed a Brand Ambassador for ABC's "The View" to represent the Mom community.

Beside her successful blog, Erica gives sales and marketing conferences for entrepreneurs and young businesspeople, speaks publicly, and mentors other entrepreneurs. Erica was the headline speaker at the 2010 National Women's Show and was also named on the list of The Top 25 Best Twitter Feeds for Women.

Additional Titles in The 99 Series®

99 Things You Wish You Knew Before...
    Facing Life's Challenges
    Filling Out Your Hoops Bracket
    Going Into Debt
    Going Into Sales
    Ignoring the Green Revolution
    Landing Your Dream Job
    Losing Fat 4 Life
    Making It BIG In Media
    Marketing On the Internet
    Taking Center Stage

99 Things Women Wish They Knew Before...
    Dating After 40, 50, and YES, 60!
    Getting Behind the Wheel of Their Dream Job
    Getting Fit Without Hitting the Gym
    Entering the World of Internet Dating
    Falling In Love
    Hitting Retirement
    Starting Their Own Business

99 Things Teens Wish They Knew Before Turning 16

99 Things Parents Wish They Knew Before Having "THE" Talk

99 Things Brides Wish They Knew Before Planning Their Wedding

www.99-Series.com